# vertical living

## Interior Experiences by yoo

**Dominic Bradbury**
**John Hitchcox**

**140 color illustrations**

# vertical living

**Thames & Hudson**

# CONTENTS

Preceding page: Artist's rendering of the Acqua Iguazu building, a yoo Inspired by Starck project in Manila, Philippines, showing a sky deck that features a rooftop pool, as well as a bar, library, movie room and terraces, with spectacular views of the city.

Opposite: The sky-garden balconies of the Lodha Evoq, in Mumbai, a yoo Inspired by Starck project.

John Hitchcox

# preface

*I*n the years since Philippe Starck and I founded yoo in 1999, the world's cities have been expanding rapidly. As our urban environments continue to grow, I believe we have important choices to make. Increased globalization offers us new and exciting opportunities to share our ideas, products, views and culture – yet the more sprawling our communities become, the more isolated we can sometimes feel. The sense of community when you live within a short distance of your birthplace; the shared local consciousness, familiarity with neighbours and sense of security and safety: these are things that have all but vanished from modern cities. With so many different geographical locations open to us today, communities are no longer focused on the village green or town hall. Instead, they are contained within the tower block. I believe that this offers us a golden opportunity to progress as a society, however; to use vertical building to our advantage and change the way we think about modern communities.

Over the years our founding vision for yoo has endured and become globally successful. Integral to this vision was our ambition to create beautiful, tempting spaces that can transform neighbours from strangers into friends. In this book we explore the idea of 'the vertical village' by visiting some of our beautiful residential projects that offer old-fashioned principles of village living within an elegant, modern setting. We also explore ways of regenerating valuable connections between people in urban locations, for instance, by designing communal areas where our residents will end up communicating with their neighbours by chance. We have worked with our impressive team of prolific and talented designers to create beautiful lobbies, stylish dining areas, swimming pools, gyms and residents' bars. These are the new community spaces – the modern-day campfires around which residents can relax, discuss the issues of the day, share ideas, interests and wisdom and watch their children grow up. By the very fact of having chosen to live in the same building, it is likely that residents will have broadly similar interests and values, which are reflected in the building's design and layout.

The principle behind yoo is to enhance lives through original design and generate communities with an emphasis on conscious living. It's been rewarding to see these values that underpin our work succeed in bringing people together. I'm reminded of a particularly nice example at yoo's Icon South Beach building in Miami, where a recording artist, an accountant and a graphic designer, who now all work together, first met over a football match in the residents' bar.

It is not only our communities that can benefit from the principles of vertical communities, but also our planet as a whole. Over the years, our presence in some thirty markets worldwide has offered us a unique insight into the changing values of our customers. Today our customers care more deeply about protecting the environment, maintaining a sustainable lifestyle and giving back to the planet. Tall buildings are more sustainable, require less real estate and have a lower overall impact on the environment than urban sprawl. Vertical living validates our desire to protect green spaces. In the coming years there will be more demand for innovations in the way we live. At yoo, we will continue to stay at the forefront, designing magnificent spaces that enrich people's lives in every possible way. There is no space more important than the home – and what better home than one surrounded by those who share your values, built with the intention of preserving our world for generations to come?

**Your home is the most important purchase you will ever make by far. It's the most important place in your life.**

John Hitchcox

**Left:** The Manhattan skyline as seen from the welcoming roof garden of The Jade, designed by Jade Jagger for yoo.

**Overleaf:**
**p. 10:** The communal 'Gold Room' lounge at Downtown, a yoo Inspired by Starck project occupying the former J. P. Morgan headquarters near Wall Street in Manhattan.

**p. 11:** In the reception area at yoo Pune, India, a yoo Inspired by Starck development, vibrant pictorial imagery brings drama and character.

# introduction

# introduction

O ur great cities have magnetic personalities. They have long attracted incomers looking for fresh opportunities and the chance to play a part in vibrant communities focused on exchange and creativity. For the city is the birthplace of new ideas, a place where minds meet and invention and innovation are pushed forwards and brought to fruition. They are centres not only of learning and culture but also of commerce and trade. As cities such as London, Hong Kong, Paris and New York have expanded, grown and renewed themselves, their character has become ever more sophisticated and diverse. Everything you could ever want and more is close at hand, with an international mix of influences and identities that bring a multi-layered quality to the metropolis. To be at the centre of a great city is to feel at the heart of the world.

Yet as our cities have grown and evolved, another side to city living has become more and more apparent and even at the epicentre of the metropolis it is more than possible to feel isolated and alone. The 21st-century city can be daunting, especially for newcomers, and it can be difficult to find a place within a society that moves at such a fast and frenetic pace. In the city your closest neighbours may be strangers rather than friends. In a traditional apartment building we might pass other residents on the stairs but have no sense of who they are or where they are heading. The great irony of the digital age is that even as a rich variety of virtual networks have sprung up, offering connectivity and engagement, we can find ourselves more isolated than ever from reality and enduring personal relationships. There is an increasing temptation to retreat into an insular, virtual world of digital networking, electronic gaming and screen time.

The vertical village, sitting at the heart of the city, is a thoughtful response to this need to build a more meaningful sense of community and foster connections between like-minded neighbours. While serving as the cradle of a fresh communal spirit, the vertical village has redefined the familiar concept of home. Home is no longer seen as simply the private space behind closed doors, but as the village itself, which offers not only a private retreat from the dynamic pace of urban life but also countless opportunities for interaction with friends and neighbours. With its communal lounges and bars as well as outdoor terraces, verandas and gardens, the vertical village is an urban oasis. There are games rooms and gyms, and perhaps a squash or tennis court, as well as more contemplative spaces such as libraries and quiet rooms. Children and families

**The pool terrace at yoo Panama, a yoo Inspired by Starck building in Panama City, offers panoramic views of the downtown skyline.**

are served with playrooms and crèches. A striking entrance lobby helps to establish the identity and character of the village, while providing a welcoming meeting point.

This sophisticated form of urban village borrows many ideas and services from hotels, but where hotel living tends towards anonymity, the vertical village fosters long-term personal connections between residents that serve as an antidote to urban isolation. A friendship might begin over something as trivial as a game of ping-pong or banter exchanged in the gym. As well as deepening the social experience of being part of a community, the presence of so many services and amenities on our doorstep, contained within the newly extended boundaries of 'home', vastly improves the quality of our daily lives. We are far more likely to use the gym or pool if it's right on hand. Relaxing with our children or talking with a neighbour seems so much easier if a tempting lounge or game-room is just a few steps away. Such positive temptations are a key way in which the vertical village is designed to improve and enhance the experience of city living.

Apart from its important social and communal benefits, the other key driving force behind the rise of the vertical village is environmental sustainability. As our cities have grown over the centuries, and especially since the mid-20th century, they have spread outwards, consuming more and more land. To look at a city like São Paulo or Mexico City is to see a metropolis that has grown too much and too fast, with overstretched infrastructure, traffic-choked roads and a lack of green space. These are cities that are quite literally grinding to a halt even as they continue to spread outwards into the surrounding countryside, swallowing forests, farmland and smaller towns and villages.

**1: The chandelier in the reception area of Downtown in New York City was found in crates in the basement of the former bank building and lovingly reassembled to form a dramatic focal point.**

**2: This apartment at Barkli Virgin House in Moscow features a bespoke library wall designed by Kelly Hoppen.**

Within older cities such as London, New York and Paris, many brownfield sites have been reclaimed for use and former industrial buildings converted or replaced with new homes. Yet the pressure for growth still remains, as the charms and opportunities of the city continue to exert their allure. Increasingly, we have begun to realize that the only way that these cities can continue to grow in a sustainable fashion is by heading upwards rather than spreading outwards.

'There is a nostalgic, romantic idea that it is more ecological to make a small building,' says Renzo Piano, architect of The Shard in London, one of the most striking of the new-generation city skyscrapers. 'Forget it – that is the worst way to consume land. This is the reason that cities grow. It's much more socially correct to intensify the city and free up space on the ground, because it's a wiser use of land. We woke up at the beginning of the new century and finally realized that the earth is fragile and must be defended. The first thing to defend is land.'

Any new tall building in a metropolis inevitably attracts some degree of comment and controversy as a consequence of its sheer height and visual impact on the skyline. Yet a sensitive, educated and creative approach to the design of new-generation, energy-efficient tall buildings is becoming an essential tool in limiting urban sprawl, conserving energy and creating more sustainable cities. These new skyscrapers also participate in the cyclical process of renewal and reinvention that is ongoing within every cityscape.

Well-designed, well-built and well-insulated tall buildings, whether commercial office space or residential vertical villages, require less energy and materials in their initial construction than is needed to build multiple smaller structures. They also cost less to maintain, and require less energy to heat and cool, saving residents money while being more friendly to the environment.

Vertical villages and other skyscrapers have many great advantages when it comes to sustainability on a community-wide scale. They are positioned in places where people really want to live, within central, downtown locations that are well served by public transport and infrastructure, as well as being close to commercial centres, restaurants, shops, galleries and other entertainment and essential services. With everything so close at hand – usually within walking distance or a short cycle away – the need for travel is vastly reduced when compared to life out in the suburbs. This is one of the great advantages of living centrally, not only because cutting down on car journeys happens to be very good for the environment, but also because it improves our overall quality of life by encouraging us to build exercise into our daily routine and removing the stress of long commutes on congested roads. The wealth of services contained within the vertical village itself further reduces the need for travel, allowing us to enjoy recreation and sport with friends and neighbours without fighting our way through the crowded city streets.

'We can build taller towers that give people plenty of space in the heart of downtown, but build them in a way that guarantees environmental sustainability and good sight lines and plenty of street life,' argues author and academic Edward Glaeser in his influential book *Triumph of the City* (2011). 'We can make sure that everybody, not just the privileged few, can enjoy the pleasures of Manhattan or Paris or Hong Kong. But to achieve all this, we must encourage cities instead of sprawl.'

High rises represent a sustainable way of providing inviting new homes and accommodating growth in older large cities, many of which are currently

**An artwork across the wall of a sitting room at yoo Pune, in India, forms a backdrop that is both playful and evocative, functioning as a vibrant focal point for the space.**

It's about wanting to be with
a group of like-minded people.

[JH]

Large floral motifs applied to both wall tiles and mirrors bring warmth to a bathroom in the Mira Moon building in Hong Kong, a Wanders & yoo project.

experiencing an important renaissance in their downtown districts. Glaeser, along with many other urbanists, contrasts this downtown revival with the gradual decline in suburban development, influenced by the rising cost of commuting by car, which, in tandem with the rise in online shopping, has also put pressure on out-of-town shopping malls and retail parks. There is renewed interest in developing more local ways of living, working and shopping, with downtown districts and historic city centres well placed to take advantage of these trends. In younger cities around the world, especially in emerging economies, towers are an important way of controlling growth, limiting sprawl and promoting sustainability.

At the same time that the design of high-rises has become increasingly energy efficient, their architecture has grown ever more creative and ambitious. From The Shard in London to Rafael Vinoly's new tower at 432 Park Avenue in New York – set to be the tallest in the western hemisphere – 21st-century skyscrapers have attained a level of grandeur and scale that sets them apart even from their most iconic forerunners.

Up until the late 19th century, the maximum height of a building was largely determined by two factors. The first was its engineering: the sheer weight of all the masonry or stone needed for construction, bearing down on the foundations and lower levels of the building, limited the safe height of most structures to approximately ten storeys. The second was practicality: before the invention of reliable elevators, walking up and down ten flights of stairs every day was more than enough to test the patience and energy of a building's occupants.

In the 1850s, however, Elisha Otis invented a new kind of elevator, which had safety locks that would hold a falling lift if the supporting cables failed. These elevators opened up a new world of verticality, especially in New York, which became the main birthplace of the modern high rise because the limited availability of land on the island of Manhattan forced architects and developers to reach for the skies. By the 1880s and 90s, advances in engineering and architecture saw a new kind of building come into the world. Load-bearing steel frames were much lighter than stone or brick structures, and strong enough to support high rises of increasing scale and grandeur. New York's Empire State Building, completed in 1931, held the record for the world's tallest building at 102 storeys and 443.2 metres (1,454 feet) high, including the spire, for forty years. The Chrysler Building of 1930, which had previously held the record for less than a year, was rather smaller at 319 metres (1,046 feet), but its Art Deco elegance endears it to many, and it is still regarded as one of the most beautiful skyscrapers ever built. The word 'skyscraper' itself was first attributed to the author Erik Larson, who used it to describe the relatively modest Montauk Block in Chicago, a ten-storey building by the architectural firm Burnham & Root, constructed in 1883 and demolished in 1902.

Load-bearing steel frames freed the walls of the building from much of their vital role in supporting the structure, as had been the case in most 19th-century masonry buildings. This led to the evolution of the curtain wall: a façade, largely of glass, that offered an open panoramic view of the city and allowed natural light to enter, transforming the whole experience of living and working in a high-rise building. By the 1950s and 60s, skyscrapers such as Mies van der Rohe and Philip Johnson's Seagram Building and Walter Gropius's Pan Am Building (now the MetLife Building) were using crisp glass façades and serving as standard-bearers for the International Style of architecture. Inside such buildings, work and living areas were increasingly open-plan as the idea of 'universal space' became common currency during the Mid-Century period.

In the latter half of the 20th century, developments in concrete construction, either reinforced internally with steel bars or used in combination with steel frames, allowed the engineering and scale of high-rises to advance even further. Most new-generation skyscrapers are now built around super-strong concrete cores that hold and protect the utility services and elevator shafts, with the floor plates radiating outwards from the core.

The image of high-rise living became tainted in the 1960s and 70s, especially in Europe, by the high-profile failures of some social housing towers, many of which had been inspired by the writings of the modernist architect Le Corbusier and his revolutionary residential developments, which he called Unités d'Habitation. The first of these, Cité Radieuse, built in Marseille in 1952, was surrounded by parkland and incorporated a rooftop running track, children's paddling pool and public terraces with views of the Mediterranean. Despite their architects' talk of constructing 'streets in the sky', however, most other high-rise towers of the period were short on the generous communal amenities and outdoor spaces that Le Corbusier had advocated in his original Unités d'Habitation.

In recent decades, however, the skyscraper has more than reclaimed its allure through a combination of vibrant architecture, expressive design and advanced engineering. Much greater thought has been given to communal spaces, and integrated gardens, terraces and balconies. The vertical village is the culmination of this new approach, embodying a fresh and more rounded way of thinking about high-rise living.

The modern vertical village is also at the heart of the work of international design and development company yoo, founded in 1999 by John Hitchcox and Philippe Starck. With a focus on homeowners' evolving needs and dreams, and keenly aware of the many different elements that form the new definition

1

## 2

1: The towers of Icon Brickell, Miami, overlooking the water; a yoo Inspired by Starck project.

2: An open-plan living space, with seating and dining areas combined and a kitchenette alongside – all with sea views – at Aqua Boracay in the Philippines, by yoo Studio.

Overleaf: This living space at the Sans Souci Hotel & Residences in Vienna, designed by yoo Studio, allows for a range of uses in one flexible space, with the master bedroom beyond.

You will end up communicating with your neighbours because they will have similar interests, which can be defined by the project and by the design.

[JH]

of 'home', yoo has played a pivotal role in developing and fine-tuning the vertical village concept, both in new-build skyscrapers and converted urban high-rises.

'We could see a strong opportunity to create spaces that would reflect the happiness of the people who live in them, forgetting the old and obsolete ideas of "home",' says Starck. 'We began spending our days dreaming up a sort of utopia, where all our friends could harmoniously co-exist.'

From the start, Hitchcox and Starck's ambition was to create a new approach to living and social space, offering choices from a palette of thoughtful, crafted design options to fit the aspirations of an intelligent, informed and like-minded group of people that Starck likes to call 'the yoo tribe'. Starck began by developing a menu of four unique interior styles (Culture, Classic, Nature and Minimal) that offered buyers a chance to shape the structure, decor and fixed elements of their own homes and apartments, with a wide range of finishes and materials. The designs are flexible enough to allow spaces to be used in many different ways, letting each homeowner's personality shine through.

Starck and Hitchcox initially worked with yoo's own design department, headed by designer Mark Davison, to serve yoo's first clients. Later, as the firm evolved and grew, other leading figures from the world of design joined the yoo family: Marcel Wanders, Jade Jagger, Kelly Hoppen and Steve Leung. Each brought with them a distinctive design approach and developed their own stylistic menus, while the choice was expanded further with the addition of new palettes created by Davison and the yoo design team. This wide choice

**1: Canopied loungers sit on the surface of the swimming pool, awaiting the residents at yoo Nordelta in Nordelta Tigre, Buenos Aires, a yoo Inspired by Starck community.**

**2: An intimate relaxation zone in the spa at the Sans Souci Hotel & Residences in Vienna.**

of interior looks are united by their emphasis on contemporary design, and their thoughtful planning and layouts.

From Europe to Asia, North Africa and the Americas, yoo has worked on a wide range of innovative projects that share common values and design themes even as they respond creatively to the nuances of each location and context. Great thought is given not just to the interiors of the individual apartments but also to the shared amenities and core qualities that set these new communities apart. Regardless of location, all yoo buildings are designed with the crucial goal of bringing their inhabitants together within a single vertical village and encouraging interaction between like-minded people.

'We are living in a society that has become more and more divided,' says Starck. 'That's why it's very important to bring people together and, yes, the way that you make a building definitely can help in this. It's simple. First, you have to make a building that is very personal. This way people feel at ease; they feel that they share the same place and the same values with the other people who live in the building. So if you make a gym, a library, a big table, some sort of place where people can meet and have a birthday party for their children or watch a movie together, then it definitely helps. To make a village you need communal spaces.'

In this way the vertical village answers a very pressing need within our cities for a greater sense of community and for a more meaningful way of living in the high-density urban environment. Instead of remaining strangers passing one another on the stairs, our neighbours become friends – people with whom we want to share time rather than simply sharing space and an address.

**The Icon Brickell in Miami features a generously scaled spa, with a vast chandelier floating over relaxation pools and an open library to one side, arranged around an open fireplace.**

# A lobby should be warm, homely, comfortable. But there should also be an element of theatre.

**John Hitchcox**

A vibrant red reception desk stands out amidst a palette of frosty whites, including a striking ceiling light, at Barkli Park in Moscow, a yoo Inspired by Starck project.

# grand
# entrances

# grand entrances

*I*n the home, as in life, it is always important to make an entrance with style. The entrance lobby plays an essential role in defining the character, depth and identity of a building. It sets the tone for what should be the start of an engaging journey from the communal threshold to your very own private sanctuary, promising many delights and surprises along the way. Too many traditional high-rise apartment and office buildings create a dull first impression with lobby spaces that are functional and anonymous.

'Vidal Sassoon said that there's only one chance to make a first impression and that's at the entrance,' says Marcel Wanders. 'Functionally the entrance is nothing, but of course it says everything about the place that you have arrived at and the people who live there. It's an entrance that you share with others and something that you pass through every day, so it should be a gift that you give to yourself. It's part of the theatre of life that should make you feel that you are arriving in a unique and special spot, made for you. Ultimately it is an expression of identity.'

The entrance lobbies of well-designed vertical villages are infused with theatrical touches and a generosity of spirit, with particular thought given to what these spaces say about the setting and character of a place, as expressed through their architecture and interior design. They are a powerful opening chapter to the design narrative and have to grab and engage the reader from the outset.

The luxurious scale and proportion of such lobbies invites a distinctive and sophisticated approach, with a high degree of drama. They take lessons from the elegant and considered welcomes provided by hotels and private members' clubs. But yoo's designers are also careful to remember that while a hotel or club might have aspects in common with an apartment building, the latter needs to provide a very particular kind of welcome. It is the introduction to a collection of homes, to a community, and must convey a sense of place and reflect the values of the people who have settled there. There may be touches of theatre at the beginning of the design story that gently threads its way through the building, but a lobby should never feel overbearing or intimidating. As a space that residents pass through each and every day, the entrance area always has to feel inviting and enticing. In some ways this is easier to achieve in an apartment complex, where such spaces are liberated by having fewer of the purely functional aspects of hotel lobbies – such as check-in desks and banks of receptionists – as well as

**Opposite: At the Dwell95 building in New York City, a yoo Inspired by Starck design, rich finishes, atmospheric lighting and a long carpet lead the way from the reception area to the elevators.**

**Overleaf:**
**p. 32: Mirror-tile walls and space-age lighting lend playful glamour to the lift lobby of The Jade in New York, by Jade Jagger for yoo.**

**p. 33: At the Mira Moon in Hong Kong, by Wanders & yoo, richly patterned mosaic floors, sculptural lighting fixtures and mirrored walls bring distinctive character to the entrance lobby.**

less traffic. The differences may be subtle but they are important: this is the doorway to the village and that door should always appear open and welcoming.

Philippe Starck stresses the importance of creating not only a grand entrance but also one that establishes the essential difference between the more 'public' spaces within a building and the private retreat that is your own apartment. 'The private has to be very calm, very serene,' says Starck. 'With the public areas, it's the opposite. You have to make something very, very strong. When the guy leaves in the morning to start his working day – which might not be fun – we have to give him his dreams. If his own lobby can be so creative, surreal, magical and incredible, then that means he can make whatever he wants; he can be incredible, be creative, be poetic. It's very important to give him the tuning – the colour of his day – to be sparkling, elegant. Everywhere you stay for no more than one minute has to be strong; everywhere you stay for more than five minutes has to be serene.'

Although entrance lobbies are transient spaces, they have to say a great deal about a building and eloquently convey a whole series of messages about the special character and quality of the property, as well as making people feel welcome. It is, on the one hand, a kind of shop window, which invites you to step into this community in the first place. But once you are part of that community – part of the village – then its gateway has to be an area that makes you feel comfortable. It may be a place to wait for a taxi, pick up a cup of coffee, talk to a neighbour or meet a friend. All of these activities are transient, yet all are staged within a space that is rich in narrative and visual power while providing a key part of the regular daily experience of the building.

A mean hallway, cluttered with post and litter, tells you something about an address: it implies that it is unloved; that the residents have little pride in their building. A generous entrance, on the other hand, one that is beautifully designed and well cared for, suggests the opposite. Here is a building that the community loves and is so proud of that they want to keep it fresh and engaging. It is a shared showcase for the character of the village itself.

1

1: Period-style furniture and a glass chandelier contrast with crisp, contemporary finishes in the lobby of seventy5Portland in Toronto, by yoo Inspired by Starck, while green planting softens and warms the space.

2: The communal areas at Lodha Fiorenza in Mumbai, by Jade Jagger for yoo, are full of playful vitality and colour; vibrant pods provide intimate spaces for meeting and talking.

In the reception area of
Barkli Park in Moscow,
a long, enveloping bespoke
sofa topped by a crystalline
light fixture suspended from
the ceiling creates a focal point;
the diaphanous curtains that
surround it feature a subtle
tree-branch pattern.

Given that an entrance lobby has to convey so many messages, it is no surprise that architects and designers put so much effort and energy into making them appealing spaces full of identity and originality. Each building demands a completely fresh design approach to its entrance area, one that not only reflects the building's local setting and context, but also creates a unique atmosphere that conveys the overall flavour of a particular community.

A building in the heart of a hard-working city such as New York, Hong Kong, Miami, Moscow or London demands a particular aesthetic, perhaps one that gives a feeling of escape and a sense that by stepping into the community you are entering a unique building that is not only welcoming but also an oasis of calm – an antidote to the fast pace of life in a hectic metropolis. A vertical village in a resort town such as Puerta Vallarta or Marrakech, however, might demand an alternative approach, reflecting its more relaxed, informal and seductive spirit.

Two very different yoo Inspired by Starck projects in Miami underline how individual the design process is for each entrance lobby. Both Icon South Beach and the Icon Brickell were created as vertical villages, each offering a wealth of communal resources, including swimming pools, gyms and other tempting spaces. As befits such a dynamic city as Miami, their lobbies have strong visual power and many theatrical elements. Yet each of the two spaces has a clearly defined identity all of its own.

Icon South Beach is set within the city's nightlife and entertainment zone, a place of high energy and excitement. Here, Philippe Starck and the yoo team created a generous lobby that is brought to life by drama of scale, with its high ceilings and sweeping sense of space. Yet this is also a calming and sophisticated entrance, a cool and evocative space with polished limestone floors and a vast chandelier partially framed by sweeping, diaphanous curtains. In front of the chandelier sits a vastly elongated reception desk – one of the longest in the world. Together they form a striking composition infused with seductive playfulness that draws you in, creating a landmark picture-postcard image that helps to define the whole community. To one side a giant golden urn disguises both a supporting column and a coffee point. A lounge area nearby is arranged around a fireplace, surrounded by a reflective wall of mirror and sitting on an illuminated glass floor. There are touches of surrealism and fantasy here, and an interplay of scale that creates a dreamlike sense of wonderment. It is undoubtedly a strong space, but also one that is elegant, fresh and full of light.

The approach at Icon Brickell offers a very different narrative. This is a large development of 1,855 apartments across two towers, situated close to the ocean. Here there is an outdoor pool, a billiards room, a library, a spa and an outdoor terrace arranged around a giant overscaled fireplace. The main lobby evokes the youthful, cinematic energy of Miami at night, creating the atmosphere of

**The lobby at Icon South Beach in Miami, a yoo Inspired by Starck project, features an elongated reception desk; wraparound curtains framing the floating chandelier add to the sense of theatre.**

an urban club, yet with a dreamlike quality. Long yellow benches criss-cross the moodily lit room, while a fireplace flickers to one side; for Starck the idea of the hearth as a homely and social focal point is an important motif, revisited in many yoo projects. The lobby is an unexpected surprise and forms a vivid contrast to both the sunlit brightness of daytime Miami as well as other, much lighter, spaces within the building; whether entering or exiting, you pass from darkness into light. There is a clear journey to be made through the building, as you proceed through a series of contrasting spaces with different flavours. Beyond the lobby, the experience changes radically as you enter sleek, white, futuristic corridors and a separate elevator zone with a mirrored ceiling.

'For me, public space is not just a lobby where you open the door, take the elevator, or get your mail,' says Starck. 'The lobby is the frontier between inside and outside and must clearly show that you are at home. It's important that people feel the frontier. For me, it's better when people say, "Oh, I live in the building with the copper roof" rather than "in Building 1325". In the old days, we never used numbers. You were the guy who lived close to the river, or the guy who lived at the crossroads – it was more human.'

At the Barkli Park tower in Moscow, the lobby is dominated by a crystalline Windfall chandelier, like a shower of falling ice. The entire space is light, crisp and elegant, with birch tree trunks and branches woven into long curtains that provide a backdrop to vast, oversized Venetian-style mirrors. In this wintry, fairytale-like space splashes of colour stand out all the more, with a translucent

1

**1: A detail of the lobby at Icon Brickell in Miami, by yoo Inspired by Starck, an inviting, warm and atmospheric composition with low-level lighting that gives it the feel of a nightclub.**

**2: Photomontage and vibrant colours enrich the journey through the communal spaces of Icon Brickell; large-scale photographic and pictorial elements are often employed to dramatic and surreal effect in yoo Inspired by Starck projects.**

It's a place where everyone in the village can meet with a sense of comfort and a sense of style.

[JH]

# You step across the threshold and you have this instant feeling of character and warmth.

[JH]

In this reception area at yoo Pune in India, a yoo Inspired by Starck complex, artwork and characterful touches, such as the assemblage of hats between the mirrored panels, stand out against the neutral walls and marble floors.

red reception desk in coloured glass and red patterned floor tiles around the lift area. There's also a generous seating area, with a long wraparound sofa filling the tempting lounge space.

'The big bench seat was covered with silver ponyskin so that it would be tactile and warm,' says Mark Davison, yoo's head of design, who worked on the space with Starck. 'But we also wanted it to look as though it had been carved out of a piece of ice. We wanted a very clean, pristine and surprising space. We didn't just want to make it all dark and warm and cosy – we wanted an antidote to that. The whole room is lined in crystalline white stone, like chunks of white sugar. You get this sense of it being made with ice.'

At Dwell95 in New York, the approach was again very different. Here the apartments are rented rather than owned and the residents tend to be younger and more sociable. The design is more playful and theatrical, alluding to the fact that the building is close to Wall Street with its tongue-in-cheek money-market references embedded in the golden reception desk, above which hangs a statement chandelier. There is a distinctly hotel-style buzz, reflecting the more transient and energetic nature of this community. A golden luggage trolley sits to one side, while a sequence of chandeliers and a vast mirror lining one wall opposite the elevators infuse the lift zone with a spirit of stand-out glamour. Other playful touches include the golden postal boxes in the nearby mail room that climb up to the ceiling.

'With our entrances we really pick up on the context and the sense of place,' says Davison. 'That's why they are all different. Each one is unique. In urban situations the emphasis is generally on creating a respite, a place to calm down from the city, but sometimes we will do something more unusual, like Dwell95. Philippe and yoo are very keen that there is some narrative in the way that you experience the lobby – and also in how you are taken through the building until you arrive at your own front door.'

Such gateways play an important role in providing the primary focal point for any urban village. They are thoughtful, considered spaces that set the tone and begin the story. They help to unite the community around a theme and a set of ideas that reflect the context and character of the village. But they are only one part of the communal area of the building as a whole – the first element in a large array of enticing spaces that help to bring residents together and that provide a backdrop to the daily social life of 'the yoo tribe'.

**Opposite: The mail room at Dwell95, a yoo Inspired by Starck building on Wall Street in New York City, plays with the banking heritage of the area, with its collection of golden mailboxes in a vault-like space.**

**Overleaf: A dreamlike lounge was created around a fireplace, on an illuminated glass floor to one side of the reception area of Icon South Beach, a yoo Inspired by Starck design.**

**The dream aspect should
be there, but the design
should also recognize
a level of permanence.**

[JH]

Philippe Starck

**P**hilippe Starck is perhaps the best known and most celebrated contemporary designer working today. He has designed a wide range of products, furniture, lighting and home fixtures for companies including Baccarat, Cassina, Kartell, Alessi, Flos, Duravit and many others. He has also designed cars, yachts, bicycles and motorbikes. His interiors and architectural projects include many hotels, restaurants and stores around the world. He co-founded yoo with John Hitchcox in 1999.

**What was the very first successful product that you designed?**

I recall a huge inflatable structure I designed for the charity Perce-Neige for the Salon de l'Enfance. It took up all the space in the Grand Palais. I was still at school when this was featured on the midday news in France.

**If you had not become involved with design, interiors and architecture, what other profession do you think might have attracted you?**

I really would have loved to serve my community as a scientist or a music composer – someone who can either save lives or change lives.

**To what extent has your approach to design evolved or changed significantly over the course of your career?**

I never was interested directly in design or architecture. It's more that I was chosen by it. I was raised with the idea that the only noble way to live was to be creative. My father was an aircraft engineer and an inventor, so the process of creating things with utmost rigour felt very natural to me. You could say that I chose to begin doing this sort of work out of laziness and cowardice.

I started to create when I was at school (I was very, very young), making drawings for my teachers that would buy me some peace, as I understood nothing they were teaching. I never understood society; I felt invisible. In order to understand society and to survive, I decided to create objects that were also means of expression and able to pass on a message. So design is actually my political weapon. And then I had to formalize all that since we live in a society that is subject to contracts and rules.

I am not intelligent enough to change. My philosophy and my ethics remain the same. If anything, I've become more radical over time and less and less interested in materiality: I prefer to help my tribe through actions rather than things.

1: A detail of the communal lounge at Dwell95 in New York City; in the evening, the lounge has the atmosphere of a private members' club.

2: In the lift lobby of Dwell95, a series of Murano chandeliers lend a touch of opulence to the space.

1

**Of all the products and projects you have designed over the years, which of them gives you the greatest sense of satisfaction?**

I'd answer this more in terms of global actions than of individual products that have given me satisfaction. My whole life has revolved around the concept of democratic design. Anyone who is blessed with good ideas has a duty to share them as widely as possible. The type of design that came out of Italy after the war, by fantastic people like Achille Castiglioni, Enzo Mari and Ettore Sottsass, was very beautiful to look at, but it was also very elitist. If there is one thing I am proud of, it's that my democratic design has revolutionized the world a little bit. I was always primarily interested in improving the quality of a product and lowering the price to the extent that anyone could afford it.

**Given the diversity of your work — hotels, interiors, yachts, products, furniture — what kind of project do you like best? Or is it the diversity itself that you like best?**

I never had, and still don't have, an overwhelming desire to create things. The numerous projects I have developed have come about either in order to replace something that I think is not something we should have, or through a personal connection with someone who asks me to crystallize his or her vision. I love all my partners: to raise beautiful children, their parents must be in love with each other, and it is the same with partners regarding projects.

**What ambitions do you have for the next ten years? Are there new avenues that you would like to pursue?**

I'd like to be really useful. It is too late for me to have a job that can save lives but I can try. I love my ongoing project of creating a laboratory for fundamental research on pure creativity, with a school attached.

2

1: A lounge area at yoo Pune, in India, includes an integrated work area by the window; Starck living spaces are typically flexible and multi-functional.

2: Back-to-back sofas create two seating areas in a single space at yoo Pune; the leather club chairs add a more masculine note to the room.

Overleaf: Communal amenities at Icon Vallarta, in Puerto Vallarta, Mexico, include seating lounges, pool tables and a library encased in yellow glass.

**When and where are you at your most creative?**

My projects are spread all over the world. A lot of my furniture editors are based in Italy; some are in the US. There are architectural projects in South America and in Asia. As for where I work, for drawing (other than when I am travelling for meetings or seeing prototypes) it is mostly in remote places, such as in the middle of the sea or the forest. I have simple cabins at my oyster farm in the southwest of France, on the tiny fisherman's island of Burano near Venice and on the Spanish island of Formentera facing the infinite sea. I prefer to remain, with my wife Jasmine and our baby girl Justice, far from cars and far from mainstream thinking in order to stay fresh and bring forth the new concepts and ideas that come from within.

**I understand that you live quite simply, but have a number of houses around the world. Where do you feel most at home?**

Anywhere, as long as I am with my wife Jasmine, the person I love. We're together on an aeroplane almost every day, so we don't really have a proper home. The clouds are our home.

**How challenging has it been for you personally to remain focused on your work while having to deal with the general tendency in our society to create a brand or a cult of personality around designers?**

I never had any ambition, or a career plan. I have always worked a lot and I still do. I dedicated my life to this sickness called 'creativity'. I proposed alternative options and my sentimental tribes decided to go for it or not. So everything became very organic, very fluid, and I never had any plan to become a brand. The 'starck' universe was self-designed year after year through my ethics, visions and projects.

**How has the experience of building yoo with John Hitchcox differed from the other projects that you have worked on and developed over the years?**

Fifteen years ago I was approached by a very persistent Englishman, John Hitchcox, who today I am very happy to call my dear friend. He approached me with a proposal to collaborate with him to create an incredible concept that would change the way we live and encourage us to thrive and be inspired by our environment.

Since I have never been interested in architecture – concrete, steel, wood – I was not eager to go ahead. But after several months of deliberation I finally accepted this partnership as I could see an opportunity to create spaces that would reflect the happiness of the people who live in them, forgetting the old and obsolete ideas of home. John Hitchcox and I began spending our days dreaming up a sort of utopia in which all our friends could harmoniously coexist. As its creators we envisioned extraordinary spaces where people could contentedly live and play. And we created yoo because, literally, it's all about you.

**What, for you, makes yoo unique?**

yoo is a very unique concept. It allows members of our tribe to be treated with competence, honesty and tenderness at a very crucial moment of their life: the purchase of their apartment. I refuse to design private homes because I want to avoid having such a high level of designer influence on someone's private and personal life. I prefer to reveal my own personality in my work for public spaces. However, sometimes people may need a little professional help from a 'friend' who is skilled in architecture and design. This is the role of yoo.

**How would you like to be remembered within the story – or history – of design?**

As an honest man, who tried to deserve to exist and who helped people through my creativity.

The communal lounge should be your perfect living room – a space where you can relax and meet your neighbours.

John Hitchcox

In one of the communal seating areas at Icon Vallarta, a yoo Inspired by Starck project in Puerta Vallarta, Mexico, floor tiles and touches of vibrant colour help bring the space to life.

# communal retreats

# communal retreats

O ver recent decades, the boundaries of what we think of as 'the home' have expanded radically. Previously, living in an apartment building meant simply that: your own home was a precisely delineated private space contained within four walls. Within a modern vertical village, however, 'home' includes not only your own apartment but also a series of diverse and inviting communal spaces within the development as a whole. These include places for relaxation and socializing, such as bars and lounges, as well as quieter retreats, including libraries. There may be dedicated spaces for families and children, such as crèches and playrooms. Added to that are leisure spaces for both fitness and indulgence: swimming pools, gyms and even spas. For its residents the building as a whole becomes 'home', rather than only one small part of it.

'I always think of it as re-creating some of the fantasy of what it might be like if you had your own palatial house,' says Jade Jagger, whose residential projects have incorporated cinemas, bars, gyms, spas, libraries and even guest accommodation for visiting friends and family. 'You would have your own cinema screening room and a shared sitting room. I love the idea of going to a bar that's in your own building. They are things that the individual living alone couldn't have, and are all the more fun for it. I think we're all looking for companionship and opportunities to get out of our own private spaces and get people together.'

Such tempting amenities bring some of the glamour and romance of a hotel stay to daily life at home, while creating a place in which you would feel very glad to spend time. With so many thoughtfully curated services available within a single vertical village, and so many opportunities to share time with friends and neighbours within your own building, there is less of an impetus to head out to gyms and cafés. It's a model for a fresh way of living in shared luxury that has an obvious and tangible appeal.

'If you live alone in a house and you want a pool, then you have to pay for it and get the cleaning right and organize everything and so on,' Marcel Wanders says. 'On the other hand, there's the concept of living in a hotel, but nobody wants to do it all the time because they want their own house or apartment. A really well-orchestrated apartment building can give you the best of both.'

**A view of the communal lounge and library at Lodha Fiorenza, in Mumbai, by Jade Jagger for yoo; libraries are standard amenities in yoo buildings, offering quiet and contemplative retreats.**

# It's all about providing a place to learn, dream and inspire – positive temptations that add value to daily living.

[JH]

Beach cabins by the water at yoo Nordelta, a yoo Inspired by Starck complex in Nordelta Tigre, Buenos Aires. Resort communities in particular are served by a wide range of communal amenities geared to leisure and recreation.

These are spaces that help bind the community together. They offer places to meet your neighbours and spend time together, rather like a private members' club. They provide areas for children to play and families to get together, all enhancing the day-to-day experience of being at home. Communal living spaces are the beautifully conceived adhesive that brings fellow apartment-dwellers into regular contact with one another, while also encouraging them to feel a sense of pride and ownership in the building itself. A building that you are pleased about and proud of is also one that you will take care of and respect.

'It really hit us how much more interesting these big buildings with amenity areas could be,' says Mark Davison, yoo's head of design. 'What we got interested in was the idea that we would encourage people to take better care of their building – these are people who are excited about the entire building and inspired to take ownership of these areas and help look after them. There are some fabulous common spaces and people do love them.

'People may have only a one-bedroomed apartment but in a sense they still own a much bigger space. They can say "I'll meet you in the lounge and we can have a beer." Just that idea alone is wonderful and that's how you get people to have a sense of ownership in the whole building.'

Tempting amenity spaces within residential high-rise buildings provide real value for money, while connecting with the design narrative of the project as a whole. But they are also an important way of addressing the increasing anonymity of city living, a phenomenon seen around the world, from New York and Paris to Hong Kong.

'In my younger days we used to know all the neighbours and all the children from different families would play outside together,' says yoo creative director Steve Leung, who is based in Hong Kong, where he also grew up. 'But lifestyles today have changed a lot and people have become more self-centred. They always use the excuse that they are busy or they may say that they are looking for privacy. But that's not totally accurate – I believe that people are the kind of animals who need to live together.

'So as a designer or an architect we should encourage people to socialize with one another and to communicate. That's why it is becoming more and more important to have some form of communal space – otherwise people become machines. Clubhouses in residential developments allow people to get to know each other and build a sense of community. They may want to bring their children or even their guests to the clubhouse for entertaining, to use the swimming pool, or to enjoy a massage in the spa. So when we talk about designing an apartment building, it's not only about the apartments themselves but also the relationship between the different apartment users and the different inhabitants of the village.'

The nature and design of communal amenities does vary by location. Resort villages often have a higher concentration of play, game and leisure spaces than do city buildings. There is also a balancing act in achieving the right number of purely social spaces alongside quieter, more contemplative spaces such as libraries and reading lounges. These calm retreats are important in that they give residents the opportunity to enjoy a carefully curated space beyond the walls of their own apartments without feeling constant pressure to socialize.

**Opposite: A children's room and crèche at Icon Vallarta. Children's areas are an increasingly important aspect of vertical villages.**

**Overleaf: In a lounge at the Kameha Grand Hotel in Bonn, Germany, designed by Marcel Wanders, a semi-circular sofa is topped with one of Wanders's iconic Zeppelin lights for Flos.**

The whole concept of sharing activities, amenities and time with your family, as well as friends, is very important.

[JH]

Shared amenities have a positive impact on our daily lifestyles in other, more subtle ways. We are far more likely to use a gym, pool or spa if it is right on our doorstep, thereby reaping important benefits for our physical fitness and general wellbeing. The presence of a childcare facility (for instance, in yoo Downtown in New York and yoo Istanbul) or, elsewhere, friendly neighbours who are willing to look after the children for an hour, make it much easier for parents to make the most of the gym. Another important benefit of shared amenities is that they do away with the need to spend time and energy commuting to use a standalone health club or finding a suitable place to meet up with friends. In large and complex cities, especially where public transport is poor and roads are clogged, this can make a very real difference to the quality and tranquillity of our everyday lives.

A number of yoo projects include tennis or squash courts, combining fitness and a social aspect. For some it may encourage a new sporting interest; for experienced players it's always easier to play a quick game with a neighbour rather than trying to plan a meeting with a friend at a sports club on the other side of town. Each of these things may sound almost trivial on its own, but collectively they enhance the rituals of day-to-day living and add to the sense of pleasure we take in our own home and our own community.

In Panama City, for example, yoo Panama, a landmark fifty-six-storey tower overlooking the Gulf of Panama, features a wide range of communal spaces, which offer many of the amenities that you would expect to find in a luxury hotel. For fitness, there is a gym and separate studios for yoga and pilates, as

2

**1: The spacious gym overlooks the swimming pool at yoo Wollerau, a yoo Inspired by Starck project in Wollerau, Switzerland.**

**2: The Marcel Wanders-designed spa at the Kameha Grand Hotel features saunas and steam rooms.**

well as two squash courts. A pool deck and terrace includes adult and children's swimming pools with cabanas and ocean views. There is a business centre, meeting and function rooms, and even a concierge service.

A double-height zone arranged around the entrance lobby includes a dramatic bar, designed by yoo Inspired by Starck. Warm, vibrant colours and statement chandeliers give the bar a playful, theatrical flavour. There is also a library where the interiors are more calming and restful, with a tempered colour palette and soothing lighting. Children, too, have their own play area within the building. At yoo Panama the vertical village encompasses a wide range of different experiences and atmospheres, offering each resident many choices in deciding how to use and enjoy the communal aspects of the development. Different design approaches distinguish party venues and social spaces from the quieter, more relaxed retreats or the children's zones.

'What we do is very different in every city we work in,' says Davison. 'Panama is a very big project with 234 apartments of various sizes and scales. People with families will choose to live here, so there is a big emphasis on children and providing places for them. And then other spaces are more flexible and might suit a party – when you provide great spaces and there's a young crowd in the building parties will always happen, but there are also ways of separating noise from quiet. The scale is what's so nice about it and it means you don't just have a token gym and a pool. There's a real generosity with these projects. Panama is quite an extraordinary project – there's space after space.

Dwell95 in New York is another large-scale project, with just over 500 rental apartments, and includes a fitness centre as well as a residents' lounge and a rooftop terrace, which makes the most of the spectacular views of the Manhattan skyline. Since the apartments are relatively modest in size, communal space was seen as particularly important in this project. The generously proportioned lounge, for instance, occupies the entire top floor of this converted office building. The lounge includes seating spaces, a library with a fireplace, and a breakfast zone where coffee and croissants are served every morning. Together with the roof terrace, the lounge is an important focal point for the community, in a prime space that might otherwise have been swallowed up by more penthouses.

'We went back to take a look after the project was finished and there would be someone in the library reading a book or two or three friends at the dining table having croissants,' Davison says. 'There are a series of connected spaces that give it some intimacy, so you can hide away a bit if you want to. But it's also a great break-out space where people can meet their friends. They are not just confined to their own apartments. There's a gym and a spa with a sauna and steam room and people come up and use the roof terrace in the warmer months.'

In the combined sitting room, library and media lounge at Dwell95 in New York City, a yoo Inspired by Starck complex, semi-partitioned alcoves allow for smaller gatherings and a degree of privacy.

# It's about enriching your life in ways that you would not necessarily find anywhere else but at home.

## [JH]

In Pune, India, yoo and its development partner are building 228 apartments in two nineteen-storey towers arranged in a horseshoe formation around lush, green parkland. Here the emphasis of the communal facilities is on relaxed indulgence, with a tea lounge, a coffee bar and a cigar lounge among the bespoke communal elements. There is also a games room, a cinema and several swimming pools hidden like jewels among the mangroves. One of the most important amenities is the substantial Six Senses spa. Complete with pools, treatment rooms and sensory escapes, the spa is largely underground to preserve the landscape.

As the development sits within tropical parkland, with many mature trees, a decision was taken to preserve as much as possible of the natural setting, which is envisaged as an important amenity for the village in and of itself. It offers a unique retreat in one of India's busiest cities. 'It's completely in harmony with the landscape,' says Davison of the development, 'a fantastic contrast to the city itself. To have these amenities is really a wonderful thing, especially when set in green parkland like this.'

In the resort town of Puerta Vallarta, on Mexico's Gold Coast, yoo created the Icon Vallarta in conjunction with the Related Group and architects Arquitectonica. With 340 apartments set within three towers, the character of the community is very different to that of a more urban village, and this is reflected in the design philosophy. As the Icon Vallarta is a beachfront resort property, it was important for the focus to be on a particular set of communal facilities suited to the climate and location. Chief among them was a striking and impressively scaled swimming pool, which includes a shallow wet bar for cooling off and relaxing, with chairs and tables set in the water itself. A vivid pink wall, planted with greenery, acts as a dramatic backdrop at one end of the pool while the other faces the beach itself. Terraces and verandas provide a choice of seating areas in the fresh air. There is also a spa and a gym – complete with its own daybeds alongside the running machines – as well as a library and a children's play den. The design offers touches of drama, humour and stand-out splashes of colour, while making the most of the outdoor setting with its stunning views out across the Pacific.

'This is very much a play resort and about having fun and being relaxed,' says Davison. 'Very few people live here all year round – it's more about coming for a vacation. The trees around the pool give you shade, as it can be very hot here, and help soften the space around the buildings. It is very family-oriented

A games room at yoo Nordelta boasts a custom ping-pong table and a videogame console; yoo villages often include social games for both adults and children.

and for a residential building these are extraordinary amenity spaces with some of the things that you would expect from a hotel.'

Whether located in the heart of the world's largest cities or in resort towns like Puerta Vallarta, a rich variety of well-conceived communal spaces is part of the core appeal of the new generation of high-rise apartment buildings. They provide good value and higher quality of life for residents, while playing a central role in combatting the sense of isolation that increasingly affects city-dwellers worldwide. Shared amenities will therefore always be crucial in creating welcoming and engaging communities, even as the technology and infrastructure of urban life continues to change.

'What else?' says Starck, 'My dream is to have a place where you can repair your bicycle or your motorbike. I like the idea of having a small garage where you can fix your rollerblades, your skateboard, anything like that. We will also have more and more new types of electric vehicles that will be able to be fixed and recharged by yourself. I would love a place where you could go and fix your bike and speak with your neighbour about the best tyre to get for it.'

1

1: The billiards room at Icon
Brickell in Miami.

2: The cinema at Icon Vallarta
in Puerta Vallarta, Mexico.

Marcel Wanders

**D**esigner Marcel Wanders opened his first studio in 1995, in Amsterdam. He is now one of the world's leading contemporary designers, with a broad range of products, furniture and lighting for companies such as Boffi, Cappellini, Flos, Swarovski and Moooi, which was co-founded by Wanders in 2001. His interior design projects include private residences, stores and hotels, such as the Mondrian Hotel in South Beach, Miami, and the Andaz Amsterdam Hotel, which opened in 2012.

**How did you first get involved with the world of design?**
Where I grew up as a kid there was no context of design. When I was sixteen I really loved the idea of being a landscape designer so I went to this school and everyone was wearing green boots but I didn't want to wear green boots all my life. I realized I didn't want to go to this school but I didn't know what else to do. Then somebody explained to me that there is something called design and I thought it could be nice.

I went to the Design Academy in Eindhoven and I was the last one that they took and way too young – just seventeen. At that point the Academy was not the kind of school it is today, but it was the only place where you could study design. I started studying there and after nine months I decided this is it, this is really what I want to do. And so I got really excited about the idea, but then they kicked me out. That was an interesting series of events.

**Did you have a mentor or inspirational teacher when you were studying design?**
I was very much encouraged by the idea that I was kicked out of this school. It was such a powerful thing for me. I really

wanted to become a designer and I understood that if I was going to become a designer it only made sense to become one of the best designers – otherwise it's nothing but a nice job. I wanted to make sure that I became really good at this and being kicked out of school gave me fantastic energy. I was furious and I was going to prove them wrong. That energy was really important.

**You work across many different disciplines of design – do you see any boundaries between them or are they all interlinked?**
I was trained as a product designer and for the first years of my career I did only this. I have been working as a product designer within a conceptual context, I guess. I really need a fantastic idea, a focus, a philosophy, a vision and only if I have this can I start the design process. The design process follows the idea, making sure that it is as clean and sharp and pure as possible. The concept will decide what the final object has to be.

It's like when you pick your piece of marble and walk around it for a thousand days and then at some point you decide what's in it and then you go get what's in it and it has to be perfect and all the rest has to be taken away. It's a process of getting to the core of things.

Later, when I decided to start doing interior design, I thought it was a logical step for me to grow as a person and as a professional, to increase the size and complexity of my universe. When I did my first projects and saw my drawings I started to think this is a really different process, because if I followed the same principles as in product design and stripped down this interior to be very clean and about one clear expression, it was going to look boring and not alive. I started to understand that an interior really is something unique and we don't expect the same things of it that we do of a product. So I started to find different ways to work on it.

Basically, where a product draws on one single, fabulous idea, the interior draws on a thousand ideas and thrives on the complexity of how all these ideas work together. That's what makes it different – it's not like sculpting a block of marble and revealing this one core thing. It's more like composing a symphony or an opera – you add and you add and you put in the flutes and then pick out the drums and the violins. It's orchestrated complexity. As I discovered this, the work became more interesting because I had to develop as a designer in a unique and different way. So I have been studying [interior design] for ten years now and I love it. It's really fantastic to have both of these typologies on my plate every day.

**What are your most important sources of inspiration?**
Inspiration is a strange and highly misused word. Inspiration for me, when I think about the work, goes back to knights in armour who fight for the goals that they believe in. They see it as an honour to serve and they are inspired by the fire that burns inside their hearts. And this will give them all the direction they need in their lives. They know why they are here and what they expect from themselves. This is not inspiration only for a day – this is who they are. That is how I feel every day about my journey. I have such fantastic challenges in my life and I am so inspired to discover what I can do, who I can serve and how I can contribute to the world. I can show what I appreciate in life and enlarge this so that everyone can enjoy it. You can tie me on a chair, put me in a room with no light, and I will still be inspired. I need nothing to be inspired.

On the other hand, I live my life as if I have a big hole on the front of my head through which everything I encounter in my life enters – all the information, all the things that people say. Around the walls of this hole are thousands of magnets and these magnets are all the challenges I face, all the things that I want to realize, the challenges I have put to myself and the quests that I am pursuing. Over time these magnets pull in all the information I need to solve certain problems.

**Your work has been described as futuristic but often refers to the past – how do you see the relationship between past and future in your work?**
When I started my design career the one thing I wanted to do was to create durable objects, objects that could serve us for a long time, and make them so great that we would never want to throw them away. So durability has always been the key to what I do and I have been investigating this. Something like twenty-five years ago I wrote a book about design and in one piece I wrote about what I called 'baby-face fixation'. We love the new so much. Our culture is so driven by a desire for change and for the new. Designers are at the forefront of liking the new, so we appreciate the work that goes into our objects but they also start to be stylized as 'new things'. So our objects have a baby-face fixation – they look very much like young babies. There is a lot of newness in it, a lot of youngness.

That's fine, but on the other hand there's nothing that grows old as fast as something new. So our objects are not made to last – they are made to disappear because they grow old when they are supposed to be forever new. So I decided many years ago that with all the projects that I do, they will have an innate respect for both the future and the past at the same time.

So when you look at the objects that I've designed, you will see that it's hard to date them. They could have been done fifteen years ago or they could have been done today, or forty years ago, or tomorrow.

### Are there any particular periods of design history that provide a point of reference for your work?

What I hear sometimes is that people call us 'baroque designers'. I always say to these people, please do me a favour and buy a book about the Baroque period because baroque is so far removed from anything that we do. We make things that are as minimal in design as I think is appropriate.

Over the past 100 years we have started to think that a space is ready when it has beautiful white walls. I think there have been so many lazy designers, or designers who don't like their job, because if you really like to design, why would you stop when you have painted a wall and think that you are finished? Why don't you make the best out of things rather than the bare minimum?

If I think about the theory behind minimalism, if I followed that philosophy when I created a gift for my daughter for her

**Above: The Moon Lounge at Mira Moon in Hong Kong, designed by Wanders & yoo.**

**Overleaf: A suite at the Marcel Wanders-designed Mondrian Hotel, South Beach, Miami.**

birthday, there I'd be with my beautiful, grey box and I'd give it to her and say this is made for you and it's as simple as possible and there is nothing to add and we didn't put a bow on it because it was more work. By the time I gave her the box she would be in the corner crying that I don't love her anymore. So I put a ribbon on the box for my daughter and I make up a fantastic story about how what's inside was packed by elves and it's the most unique object you will ever have and then I give it to her. There's nothing minimal about that. I think about how to create things that people love, which is the key to what I want to do.

**Your work in lighting design really seems to have captured the public imagination. Do you have a view on why your lights have been such a success?**
If you look at light fixtures in the present then you have to start by understanding that the functionality of these pieces is completely lost. Of course we need the light, but you can build it inside the wall, the ceilings – we find light in a material way. So the armature of light, the fixtures, are not functional.

So my approach to lighting is different to that of other designers. It's nothing to do with the technology and functionality of lighting – it has to do with the people around the lighting and how we think of lighting. I make things that people really feel they want above their table because they are sitting there with friends. Take the Skygarden light, for example – it's a fantastic light that hangs in your house in a simple, architectural way. From a distance you see a very clear, geometric shape and it works that way really well, as an object you see from afar, and then when you are sitting directly under it at the table you see that there is a bouquet, a garden, hidden inside it. So the light has architectural size and capacity but also, when you look closer, intimacy and personality.

They are very sculptural pieces. Lights can be sculptures: you don't even touch them; they are often there only for sculptural effect. But having said all this, in my studio I am also a technocrat and I make sure that the light is perfect and that it does exactly what I want it to do. It's something that I would never talk about with my audience – it's something we just get done. To my audience I want to be the poet, the magician.

**Your lighting has a very playful and optimistic quality. Are these characteristics important within all of your work?**
There's a dark side in me but I don't think that design is an area where my dark side should be expressed or shared. The art that I create, which is much more intimate, is the a perfect area for me to share other sides of myself. I think design is a place to share the positive things in life and the beautiful things in life. If I feel cynical at some point in my life then I will go home and get my act together and solve my problems before I design anything. I don't want to design unless I am feeling positive.

**To what extent did working on the interiors of the Mondrian South Beach hotel in Miami influence or affect the direction of your work and career?**
About ten years ago I decided that I wanted to do interiors and started working on small projects. I really wanted to do a hotel but thought that nobody would give me a project. I always like the idea that I can sit on both sides of the table so I started my own hotel with a friend of mine. It was very small, with only seven rooms, each of them unique. It took us a long time. It was not the typical modernist hotel – it had such a different atmosphere, warm and beautiful and rich. The images of this small hotel – Lute Suites – were published all over the world and everyone saw them. Soon afterwards we were asked to do our first real hotel – the Mondrian. For me that hotel was like the opening of a universe – it was the first full-size hotel that we had ever done, and it was for a group that is a leader when it comes to designing hotels. It was great to work with them.

I like to really evaluate what I offer. I like to buy what I sell. A lot of designers would never buy. Recently, in Amsterdam, I opened another hotel which I own, and when I designed it, it was really like sitting on both sides of the table again.

**A lounge and living room at the Mira Moon, with a choice of areas for work, dining and relaxing.**

The balcony of a suite at the Mondrian Hotel, South Beach, Miami; the generous scale of this outdoor space allows for both dining areas and a custom hot tub.

**What, for you, are the unique aspects of designing a yoo project compared to other kinds of interiors commissions?**
Our yoo projects, if you compare them to projects we do without yoo, are done as far as possible with the same spirit, the same energy. They are guided by the same values and have the same core identity. We work with a team at yoo but they want us to be us. They don't want us to be Philippe Starck or Kelly Hoppen. We work with them and help them to follow the logic of the studio. At the same time, with yoo we are able to develop designs that draw on their knowledge of international flavours and realize projects that we couldn't do alone, especially in creating apartments. yoo has the capacity to communicate in new markets and find clients who are ready to do something exceptional. We do fantastic things together and I'm very happy to work with yoo.

**We try to create an oasis garden that brings some calm, some sensory experience to the village.**

**John Hitchcox**

The swimming pool at Icon
Vallarta, a yoo Inspired by
Starck resort community
in Puerto Vallarta, Mexico,
laps at the verandas and
outdoor rooms, shaded
by the building itself.

# outdoor living

# outdoor living

*A* thriving vertical village relies on the presence of engaging communal spaces not only within the building but also outside it. Outdoor living rooms and roof gardens are becoming intrinsic and valued elements within urban developments worldwide. Designers, developers and homeowners alike recognize the powerful allure of being able to step out into the open air within the protective enclave of your own home, along with the many other benefits of both shared and private outdoor spaces.

Such thoughtful integration of outdoor living space in contemporary vertical villages represents a marked point of departure from the high-rises of the past. Roof gardens and green outdoor spaces were largely ignored by the architects of early skyscrapers, who saw them as irrelevant complications that compromised the purity of the building and were too challenging to engineer and maintain. The great skyscrapers of the 20th century still provide sources of inspiration and many have become iconic buildings in their own right. But they have also shown us that if we are going to create new and sustainable vertical villages in our cities, then we have to think more carefully about the needs and desires of those who will choose to live in these communities. Roof gardens and outdoor rooms have traditionally been seen as luxuries, but in the 21st century they are increasingly regarded as necessities, design considerations that are almost as important as space and light and integral to the spirit of a well-conceived building.

This fresh emphasis on green urban retreats and outdoor rooms is part of a radical reassessment of the way we use space in the city. Once regarded as a blank, utilitarian space – the realm of water towers, lift-shaft summits and air-conditioning and heating vents – the rooftop, for instance, is now considered a key resource that can benefit the entire community, and far too precious to be wasted on mechanical services. Rooftop terraces, bars and lounges make the most of the extraordinary views and vistas of a city, providing a dramatic vantage point over the urban expanse, while rooftop pools and gyms provide wonderful amenities for residents. The obvious practical benefits of city sky-gardens are numerous. Their planting helps to increase the green stock of the city, capturing carbon dioxide and cleaning the air. On a more subjective level, they are oases of greenery in cities of concrete, steel and glass, with intense sensory and visual appeal that makes them great sources of pleasure and wellbeing for children and adults alike.

**The generously scaled roof terrace at Downtown in New York City, a yoo Inspired by Starck project, functions as a vibrant outdoor living room at the heart of the city that can be used both day and night.**

1

1: This house, designed by Kelly Hoppen for yoo, at The Lakes by yoo in Gloucestershire, UK, features a generous deck with space for outdoor dining and sun loungers.

2: The communal areas at Icon Vallarta include this outdoor garden lounge.

Given the fact that cities can sometimes be overwhelming places in which to live and work, leaving some of us susceptible to feelings of claustrophobia and a sense of disconnection from nature and the changing seasons, gardens and green spaces are all the more important in the urban landscape. Just as we constantly gravitate to parks, fountains and pavement cafés, so we take delight in balconies, rooftop terraces, belvedere bars and alluring outdoor spaces within our own village communities. Cities that provide generous parklands and green spaces for their residents are always considered more desirable, and the same can be said for the buildings in which we choose to live. In the warmer months we have a natural need to spend some time outdoors rather be confined by four walls. The provision of outdoor space at the heart of the city, then, is always liberating: it encourages a sense of freedom that counters the claustrophobia of urban living and enriches the whole idea of 'home'.

In Asian cities where living space is at a premium, outdoor space in a high-rise development is considered even more of a precious commodity. 'Outdoor space and gardens are a real luxury in cities like Hong Kong,' says Steve Leung. 'In high buildings the penthouses that have the luxury of owning roof space or some apartments with set-back terraces will be seen as very special. Whenever we do a residential building in Hong Kong we will try and provide outdoor space for the enjoyment of residents. Outdoor space is seen as very important.'

The creation of rooftop gardens and communal green retreats is vital in cities that have little in the way of public parks and squares. Shaping these outdoor spaces, which are always integrated into the design of the building from the start, is a welcome challenge for architects and designers, offering an opportunity to create terraces, verandas and rooftop meeting places that are enticing, alluring and glamorous, infused with a sophisticated sense of modernity. They have the potential to become vibrant social spaces comparable to the rooftop gardens created by hotels and private members' clubs in cities such as Miami, Marrakech and London, where the urban skyline provides a striking and inspiring backdrop to the design.

For Philippe Starck, part of the appeal of designing such urban gardens lies in working with the engaging contrast between nature and artifice and the way that the two combine. 'When we are lucky enough to have outside space, we have to think about how people can be more happy, where people can be most comfortable, where they can meet, where the children can play and be in the shade and not in the sun,' says Starck. 'With the style, we have to create a contrast – a collision, a fight – between something very natural, and some sort of man-made surprise: a piece of a playground that looks like a sculpture, a swimming pool that resembles a natural feature or a jade sculpture. It's a mix of both. There is nothing more beautiful than encountering an expected piece of art that is set not in a manicured garden but in a real piece of nature.

'Where we are able to have them, outdoor rooms are fantastic. The most beautiful one for me is a terrace in Paris made for the de Beistegui family with the help of Le Corbusier. It was like an apartment with no roof and all the walls, the console, the closet, the fireplace, the armchairs were open to the sky and the carpet was in grass. It looks like something by Salvador Dalí. Even years later,

Pools, terraces, gardens and private balconies are all part of the outdoor experience at yoo Nordelta, a yoo Inspired by Starck community in Nordelta Tigre, Buenos Aires.

**Gardens and outdoor space encourage conscious living and being more aware of the wider environment around you.**

[JH]

The roof lounge of The Jade in New York City, by Jade Jagger for yoo, is an open-air social space looking out across the rooftops of Manhattan.

it is still the best example of how to make a garden: make it like your home, just without a roof.'

In New York, Jade Jagger's The Jade on West 19th Street epitomizes the kind of excitement that rooftop gardens can bring to a building. Here the roof becomes a key part of the social scene, with tables, sofas, daybeds and sunbeds set among green planters, while soaking tubs offer cooling dips in high summer. The scenery here is cinematic, with views of the water towers, rooftops and landmark skyscrapers such as the Empire State Building.

Another early project in Manhattan, Downtown, also makes bold and creative use of outdoor space. Here the communal spaces include a basketball court, a bowling alley, a fitness centre and a children's playroom. This project was a conversion of a former banking building once owned by J. P. Morgan. One of its most vibrant spaces is a large, elevated park, positioned over the entrance zone five storeys above the street level, on a vast terrace that overlooks the New York Stock Exchange. With water pools, benches and tables for relaxing, and trees planted in enormous terracotta pots, the park is a social hub for all the building's diverse residents. 'In the day during the summer the terrace comes alive,' says Mark Davison, yoo's head of design. 'There are parents out with their children and nannies and there are people of all nationalities. There's buzz and chatter. Then at the end of the day when the children disappear, the young girls and guys come back from work and there's noise and people having a good time. You couldn't ask for anything better.'

At the Horizon in Bangalore, India, yoo and its partner House of Hiranandani have created an extraordinary lakeside vertical village retreat complete with a gym, lounge and games room. A key element of the project is a large rooftop

**1: The broad wooden terrace of Elle Macpherson's home at The Lakes by yoo, designed by yoo Studio, features a daybed overlooking the water.**

**2: A rooftop jacuzzi offers views of the picturesque countryside at yoo Nordelta.**

We put tremendous energy and thought into what you can do within a city environment to create an urban resort with roof terraces, vertical gardens, water pools and more.

[JH]

The broad, sheltered balconies at yoo Nordelta feature outdoor kitchenette–bars and space for relaxing and enjoying views of the pools, waterways and nearby golf course.

terrace garden, with a swimming pool and sun deck, where clipped green hedges form green walls that offer shade and frame views of the city. Planted trees help to divide the space into separate seating areas, and Starck provides sculptural surprises among the greenery. Green hedging also encloses a barbecue area, with tables and fireplaces. The effect is engaging and surprising, with a touch of that Dalí-esque surrealism that so often inspires Starck's approach to outdoor living space.

'Here we needed to think about the sun and how to provide shade. We thought we could achieve that by planting these tall hedges and creating this series of individual outdoor rooms,' says Davison. 'Hedges also run along the sides of the terrace so you get views out of these hedge windows, which is a great idea. We also wanted a sculptural piece that we could drop into the pool. The idea is that water trickles down so you have the sound of running water, like a fountain.'

At yoo Pune, in India, the entire village development is arranged around mature gardens that provide a lush, green backdrop for the community. Here the village is very much an oasis within the city, sitting within grounds rich with fully grown trees and tropical greenery. 'So often we have the problem that it might be ten or fifteen years before the landscape really knits together and that's just life,' Davison says. 'But in Pune we have this incredible, ready-made paradisical garden with beautiful specimen trees, so we are very much working around that.'

Resort villages such as Icon Puerta Vallarta in Mexico and Jade Jagger's The Baglioni in Marrakech have also placed a great emphasis on outdoor living. The Baglioni features landscaped gardens arranged around plunge pools, with canopied daybeds and olive trees.

1

1: A rendering of one of the
garden rooms at yoo Nordelta,
shaded by trees and overlooking
the nearby water pools.

2: A giant fireplace and vast
screens form windbreaks to
shelter an outdoor lounge at
Icon Brickell, Miami, a yoo
Inspired by Starck design.

Overleaf: A communal balcony
lounge, with plunge pool, at
Lodha Fiorenza in Mumbai,
designed by Jade Jagger
for yoo.

In some locations it is necessary for outdoor areas to shield residents from extremes of climate. On the communal terrace of the Icon Brickell in Miami, for instance, giant screens of glass and Corten steel and a vast, oversized fireplace create windbreaks that help to shelter the seating area from the strong coastal breezes that blow in from the Atlantic. The visual effect of these ultimately functional elements is, however, endearingly surreal and successful from the standpoint of design.

Some future urban projects will offer residents the experience of near-complete immersion within the natural setting. Innovative ideas for green communal living have already been developed at The Lakes, yoo's English country village development in the Cotswolds. Here, contemporary lodges sit within a naturalistic landscape created, with the help of conservationists, around a series of lakes. This is very much a family community, complete with chickens and pet huts, wildflower meadows and orchard playgrounds, as well as facilities such as a gym and spa. There is also a vegetable and herb garden, with space for residents to do their own planting. The lakes are an amenity in themselves, used for fishing, boating and canoeing. yoo intends to transplant some of these elements to its urban vertical villages in the near future. Fruit and vegetable plots will be introduced in sky-gardens where space allows, and vertical gardens and green walls will become intrinsic to communal outdoor living spaces. Beehives and planting for birdlife can also be part of this approach. Many other opportunities remain to be explored in the quest to make the sky-gardens, terraces and outdoor rooms within vertical villages both sustainable and enticing.

**This large terrace overlooking the water, at a house designed by Kelly Hoppen for yoo at The Lakes, has space enough for a long outdoor dining table.**

Jade Jagger
& Tom Bartlett

*A*rtist, jewelry designer and interior designer Jade Jagger grew up in Paris, London and New York. She studied painting in Florence before establishing her own jewelry design studio. For many years she was the creative director of Garrard, the jewelry house. In 2009 Jagger also launched her own fashion label and opened her first eponymous store in London. She began working with yoo, in association with Tom Bartlett, in 2004.

Architect and interior designer Tom Bartlett studied at the University of Manchester and the Bartlett School of Architecture in London before co-founding the Waldo Works design studio in 2000. As well as his work for many private residences, Bartlett has designed interiors for Selfridges, Smythson and Garrard, among other corporate clients.

**What or who first got you interested in design?**

**Tom:** I trained as an architect so I went to university and decided that's what I wanted to do. Architecture, it begins with an A: top of the list. So I found it pretty exciting and then went to the Bartlett School of Architecture where I got really excited and started to design high-end residential projects and that's how I met Jade.

**Did you have a mentor figure growing up, in terms of design?**

**Tom:** My mother was always among fashion people. Her best friend was Barbara Hulanicki of Biba and so I always had that '60s aesthetic around me. And our house was endlessly changing from chocolate lacquer to bright red drawing rooms so I became quite interested in interiors early on.

**Jade:** I started off as a painter, very much in a decorative sense, loving all things beautiful, and then realized that I very much enjoyed the practical application of that as well – beauty and daily living. I did sculpture and ceramics and then I moved into jewelry. The interiors for Garrard were my and Tom's first project together and we did a number of Garrard stores in New York, London and Japan. Besides that, I've always loved the home and have put that first – the creation of a home environment.

**Tom:** I think Jade was one of the first people of my age group, when we were a bit younger, who had a proper house. She was one of the first of my contemporaries who had an interior and who was thinking about those things from really early on.

**Jade:** I travelled so much that I really got an amazing depth of experience of different cultures and the different styles and different ways in which people live. That helped to give me a broad perspective and understanding of how you might like to live. I spent a lot of time in America and I'm sure that was another major influence on my life.

The communal lounges at Lodham Fiorenza in Mumbai are rich in colour, statement lighting and playful charm, with a touch of retro-style glamour.

**How do you tend to work together on a design project and who does what?**

**Tom:** Well, the process starts when someone comes along and says they'd like to work on a Jade Jagger for yoo project. And then hopefully we'll go out to meet them. So that will be someone from the design team here, and me and/or Jade, so that we can get a brief together. Then we start the design process. The yoo studio does all the drawings; we give creative input and then we start the crit process to get ready for presentation. Either Jade or I will go out and present to the developer client once we're happy.

**And the client could be anywhere in the world?**

**Tom:** Luckily at the moment we're working a lot in India and Jade has a house in Goa. So that's quite convenient and we're just signing some new projects elsewhere, but yes, there's quite a lot of travelling involved.

**And how do you tend to spark ideas off one another?**

**Tom:** We've always riffed on the four design palettes that we created for yoo, although they do evolve. But that's the basis of our concept.

**Jade:** And I think we do look at each project individually, even though we're using similar ideas of geometry or colour. I find that they're all very inspiring individually, even if one is more particularly about a clubhouse or one is more residential. I love the collaboration.

**Tom:** The projects are very different, but there are themes that we always come back to. I don't think anyone could accuse us of giving people projects that are all the same. But thematically we're trying to keep to quite a tight concept.

**Where do you tend to find your sources of inspiration?**

**Tom:** I think India has been a constant inspiration. There has always been an interesting energy generated between the

decorative stuff that we get from India and the more architectural lines that we like to set that against. There's always been quite a contrast that India's put forward for us.

**Jade:** India has been a huge backbone of inspiration in my life because I've worked there and I feel it's a country that still has design in daily life. You see a love of creativity and an attention to detail that no other place in the world can match. Its people still have a great respect for handicraft.

**Tom:** Rather than being slightly snooty about it, as we can be in the West. It's still rather beautiful and sweet.

**In terms of your outlook on life and design, do you think you're very similar?**

**Jade:** I don't know how similar we are as people and in the way we live. Tom lives a more solitary life, whereas I have two children and millions of dogs. But aesthetically I think we look at things the same. I'm always trying to be more practical. Everybody laughs when I say that I'm the more practical side of the team, but I think maybe women usually are. They're always wondering where they're going to put their towels.

**Tom:** It's like one of those terrible clichés about a good marriage.

**And you can spar ideas off each other?**

**Tom:** Yes, without compromising. I think that's the key – that we don't compromise.

Playful sparks of wit – as in this workstation and wall-clock composition at The Jade in New York City – add another layer of charm to a space without undermining the sophistication of the overall design.

Overleaf: The juxtaposition of water towers and Manhattan skyline as the backdrop of a carefully curated outdoor room generates visual drama at The Jade.

**Are there any particular periods of design that inspire you?**

**Tom:** The reaction you get from the combination of materials is what interests me most. It's probably materiality that I look to for inspiration, if that answers your question.

**So is that often the starting point? Does that come quite early in the thinking process?**

**Tom:** It does for me, yes. In terms of finishes, we are quite touchy-feely. And colours. We always look at pattern because pattern is so interesting across cultures, trying to reinvent it and not just reuse it. But the most important thing is taste.

**So the palettes you created allow you enough flexibility to respond to a particular sense of place and then feed that back into the project?**

**Jade:** Yes, and I do think they lend themselves to either urban or country environments.

**Tom:** When we were originally thinking about these things, we were trying to think about the whole gamut… All of our style names are ironic but the idea of 'Aristo' has this slightly more heritage idea – that cult of Englishness that you find all over the world. 'Boho' is something that references Jade's house in Ibiza that we worked on together and has that Mediterranean feeling. 'Disco' is something to do with New York in the 1970s, really. 'Techno' is about the life of a jet-setter. I think we like to start with humour, basically. I think it's a very important factor. There's a sense of mothering this kind of little egg of a community that's about to start and there is a responsibility in that. It's not just about slapping your name on something.

**Of all your yoo projects, do you have a favourite?**

**Jade:** I think the first one. New York was fabulous.

**Tom:** We worked with a great team and it was just so exciting. I mean, New York. Walking up 19th Street with your briefcase in the morning, checking this huge building that you are fiddling around with. It was a joy.

**And Jade, did it feel particularly special because it was where you grew up? Was that part of it?**

**Jade:** Definitely – and it's called The Jade. Also, the fact that we created something so unique with these small spaces. We met the challenge.

**Tom:** We worked so hard on that, trying to make these very small spaces become jewel-like and function perfectly, with lots of different atmospheres, and it really worked.

**Do you have a particular definition of luxury when it comes to the spaces that you live in or work on?**

**Tom:** 'Luxury' is quite a difficult word. I think 'luxury' should be replaced with the word 'bespoke', because I think when something is made perfectly for you, that's the most luxurious thing you can imagine.

**Jade:** I think the ultimate luxury is the time you have in which to enjoy the things you've created.

**What are the common threads to the rooms and spaces that you design together, wherever they may be?**

**Jade:** I think the way we work. The way we use geometry, the way we use colour in a bold way – lots of colours, spectrums and patterns, but without turning a space into a bohemian mess. We're retaining a sense of modernity.

**Tom:** I also think that if you were really analysing it then we use very traditional furniture plans that are basically created around the need for comfort. I think the way we lay out furniture is quite specific to us.

**Do you have things going on together apart from your yoo projects?**

**Tom:** We're always fiddling around.

**Jade:** We have a possible hotel that we're doing in India. But I find it hard to do those five-year plans, because things always change. I think it's very important to be open.

Vibrant splashes of colour and pattern bring a fresh, vital quality to these enticing dining and living spaces at Lodha Fiorenza in Mumbai.

**And obviously you've got to keep your own personal projects going as well?**

**Jade:** Yes, like my jewelry, and I also do some project design. I work for Guerlain and L'Oreal. I rebranded and redesigned the perfume bottle for Shalimar, which hadn't been touched since it was first developed. In a way it's quite architectural. I've also been working with some of the old French wine houses and did a wine label for a classic Bordeaux. Other than that, it's mainly my jewelry business. I've got my store in London and I've just opened an atelier in Ibiza.

**Do you have a favourite building?**

**Tom:** Mine is the Brion Cemetery in Italy by Carlo Scarpa. Because it's one of the most poetic places, even though it's about death. It's just so beautiful and in terms of its bespoke elements the design is just awe-inspiring.

**Jade:** I think one of the buildings that most influenced me in my life was the Hermitage in what was Leningrad when I first visited, but is now St Petersburg. It wasn't only the decadence of the palace, but also its contents. This was one of the moments when I realized that I wanted to devote my life to the arts and

design. I was just overwhelmed by it all. I went when I was thirteen. It was before glastnost and perestroika. The Hermitage was hanging on by a thread but stacked full. I insisted that my school went there because I was so obsessed with Russian history.

**Are you happiest in town or country?**

**Jade:** The country. I find the peace and silence and closeness to nature to be one of my greatest inspirations, certainly for its colour and natural beauty. I find that time feels much more open there and that the distraction is the right kind of distraction. But I also think the city is great for influence and interactivity. It's great for culture. I live on the South Bank and I love being right there next to everything, the Tate, the Hayward... But I definitely work better in the country.

**Tom:** I like the country for various reasons. I understand it. I'm quite solitary. I grew up in London, but I also grew up in Wales and Connemara, in the west of Ireland. I say the country, but I'm quite split, really. There are different needs. But I do like a bit of rain and a bit of lichen and a bit of coming in to a fire. I find that very appealing.

The thing about open-plan living is to try to preserve some cosiness.

John Hitchcox

Light, spacious and comfortable open-plan living at yoo Pune in India, a yoo Inspired by Starck design.

# open-plan living

4

# open-plan living

*T*he way we live has shifted greatly over the past fifty years. Our increasingly informal and open lifestyles have seen a radical transformation in the way that our homes are planned, arranged and ordered. The Victorian idea of the home as a series of individual compartments, each with a clear purpose and identity – dining room, sitting room, kitchen, study, and so on – now seems a world away from the manner in which most of us want to live today.

This process started gathering pace in the 1950s. In the mid-20th century a number of pioneering modernist designers and architects, such as Mies van der Rohe, Philip Johnson and Richard Neutra, developed the idea of the 'universal space', or open-plan living. Under their influence, the boundaries between the traditional, compartmentalized rooms began to dissolve in favour of a more relaxed and fluid floorplan, accompanied by a similar erosion in the division between indoor and outdoor living spaces.

Instead of a warren of individual rooms, we now had a more general distinction between 'private' and 'public' spaces within the home. The former consisted of bedrooms, bathrooms and other intimate spaces. The latter was an open-plan or semi-open-plan living space that combined areas for seating and dining, alongside an integrated kitchen that might be partially divided off by kitchen counters or the arrangement of furniture and storage.

Such a way of living seems almost standard to us now, in an era when even period homes tend to be adapted to take account of open-plan living patterns. But in the mid-20th century the concept of 'universal space' was a radical shift in both architecture and personal values. It reflected the more liberal and casual way of life in the post-war world within a spirit of futurism, reinvention and 'making it new', coupled with a consumer spending boom in the late 1950s and 60s that helped to energize the design and marketing industries.

By the 1980s the shift towards open-plan space was taken further with the trend for 'loft living', which began in New York and London but was soon emulated internationally. Former warehouses and industrial spaces were converted into wide, open living spaces, sometimes with no partitions at all apart from bathrooms, with sleeping platforms or open bedrooms incorporated into a single expansive space. Different 'zones' for dining, sitting, sleeping and working were defined more by the arrangement of furniture and shifts in floor levels or flooring materials rather than by solid boundaries.

**This open-plan living space created by Kelly Hoppen for yoo at The Lakes by yoo in Gloucestershire, UK, encompasses a comfortable seating area and a generous dining table, with a fluid connection to the adjoining outdoor living space.**

# Open-plan is great for communication.

## [JH]

An open-plan communal lounge at The Jade in New York City, designed by Jade Jagger for yoo, features a choice of areas for sharing time with family and friends, while connecting easily with the roof terrace alongside it.

A number of yoo's principal designers, including Mark Davison, were involved in pioneering developments in the 1980s and 90s that explored the nature and character of loft living. Today, its design philosophy is rather different, with the goal of achieving a considered balance between open-plan spaces and private sanctuaries within the home. This requires shaping spaces that are fluid and open on the one hand, allowing easy communication and circulation, but that also feel welcoming, enticing and engaging.

This approach to crafting living space is guided by the twin notions of 'sophisticated simplicity' and 'informal elegance'. The choice of aesthetic palettes created by Philippe Starck, Marcel Wanders and other yoo designers promote a degree of simplicity, a sweeping-away of clutter within a strong and clear floorplan and a thoughtful structural arrangement. Living spaces offer a welcome level of integrated and practical storage that helps clear away some of the physical detritus of everyday living, placing an emphasis on the provision of living areas that are not only appealing, but also functional and practical. They provide a clear framework for daily living and serve as the strong foundations on which the individuality and character of each apartment can develop organically.

'It's important that your home is somewhere that you can nurture your family, be with friends, a place that totally functions around your needs,' says Mark Davison. 'We can make it look fabulous, too, but more important are the bones that lie underneath it.'

An ample provision of storage is essential, with a wealth of wardrobes and cupboards, along with utility spaces, even in smaller apartments. There is an understanding that as well as being a home, this apartment may also be a place

1

1: Inviting alcove seating – a variation on a window seat – graces this television lounge at Lodha Evoq in Mumbai, a yoo Inspired by Starck design.

2: This open-plan space at yoo Berlin in Germany, a yoo Inspired by Starck design, combines a lounge and dining area in a single universal space, while the kitchen is partially partitioned off to the rear.

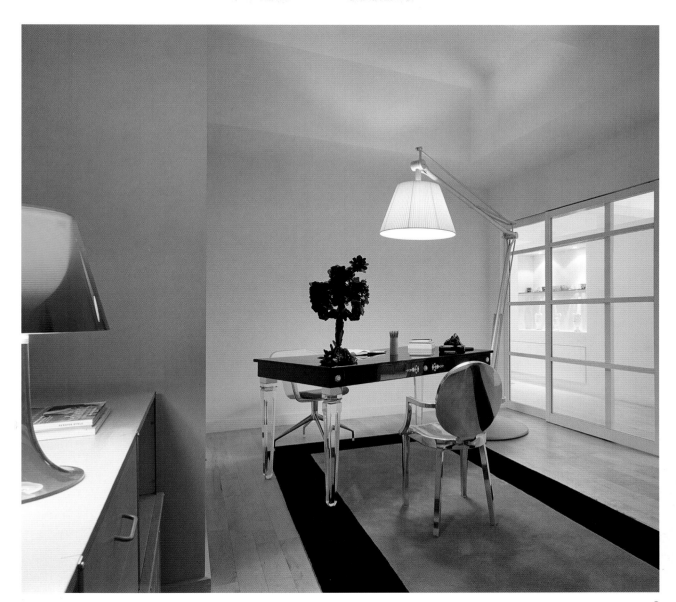

1: This indulgent open-plan living space at Barkli Park in Moscow, created by yoo Inspired by Starck, includes comfortable corners as well as the main seating and dining areas.

2: The fact that many of us now choose to work from home, at least part of the time, is recognized in the inclusion of study areas and workstations, as seen here at Downtown, a yoo Inspired by Starck building in New York City.

of work, as more and more of us choose to work from home. Living spaces are designed to offer a choice of areas for this purpose, for instance, with integrated workstations and extra cupboard space for hiding away paperwork and computers.

The common principles that underlie this flexible approach to living space are reflected in vertical villages around the world, from Tel Aviv and Berlin to Panama. At Barkli Virgin House in Moscow, designed by Kelly Hoppen for yoo, the apartments have a typically expansive feel. The generous proportions and high ceilings of a large open-plan living area, with opulent finishes and fine detailing, encourage the eye to wander, giving an impression of space and volume. Within city-centre developments, where space itself is seen as a luxury, this impression is enhanced by the openness of the key living areas and the way in which the floor-to-ceiling windows provide a high quality of natural light, adding to the overall sense of spatial generosity and delight.

At Barkli Virgin House subtle devices and measures are used to separate the space into different zones without disturbing the overall sense of scale. At one end of an apartment a seating area sits next to a library wall; a shift in floor material from polished stone flags to stained timber helps to define the boundaries of this sitting zone. A folding and semi-translucent screen separates the sitting zone from the dining area alongside the kitchen, which also reads as

**1:** At this house created by the yoo Design Studio at The Lakes by yoo, the kitchen and dining area flows directly into the living room, yet the lounge is clearly demarcated by the arrangement of furniture and changes in flooring materials.

**2:** At Lodha Evoq in Mumbai, the sitting area, dining zone and kitchen harmoniously coexist in a single space.

It's about creating space that allows interaction – we're social animals. We like to spend time together and open-plan living facilitates that.

[JH]

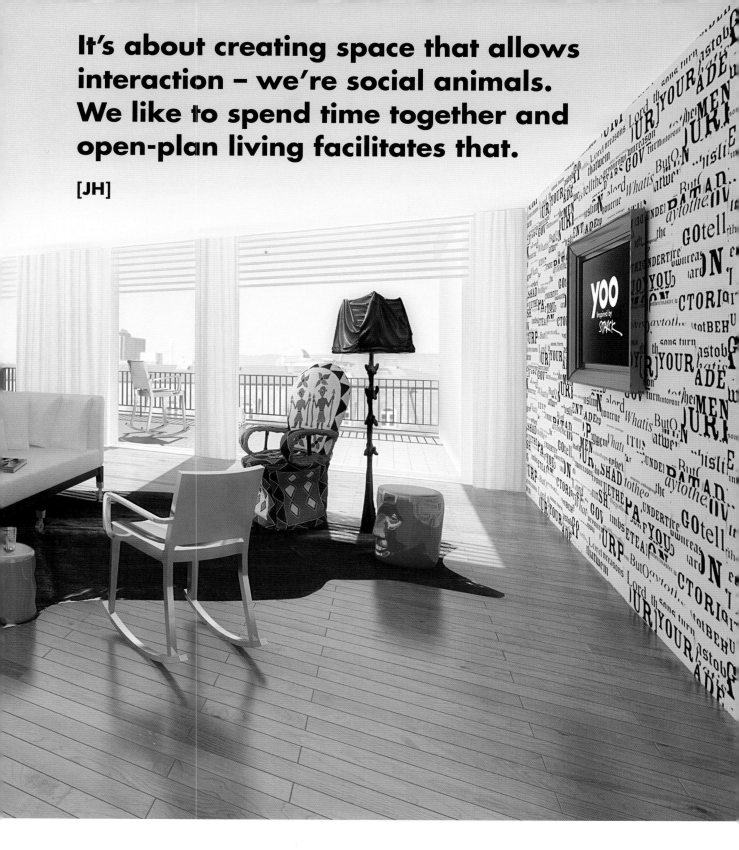

part of the space as a whole but is contained by a long kitchen counter and another shift to wooden flooring. The use of reflective wall surfaces and mirror glass helps light to circulate and enhances the feeling of spaciousness, while contemporary glass chandeliers add another diaphanous and ethereal element.

Mirrors and mirrored glass are commonly used in yoo projects to add to the quality of light and the perception of volume in a room. 'Mirror is a great way to create an illusion of depth and space,' says Jagger. 'It can help a room in many ways and is useful for drawing the eye and creating a focal point.'

The open-plan approach helps to create a more social home, a place where communication between family members and friends becomes easier and freer. This is an important principle in all yoo developments, also reflected in the design of communal lounges and social spaces that encourage greater interaction between friends and neighbours.

'We really do believe in that mixing of living, cooking and dining in one space,' says Davison. 'We think it's vital and a way of keeping that constant connection between family members. We don't want kids in one room on their phones, Mum in the kitchen or lounge and Dad in the study. If you have family or friends with you, then you want to be together – you don't want to separate out into different rooms.'

The Lakes, in the English countryside of Gloucestershire, is a yoo community that has generated many ideas that are filtering outwards into other developments, both rural and urban. This contemporary Cotswolds village features individual houses by Kelly Hoppen, Jade Jagger and Philippe Starck, with many shared amenities. Elle Macpherson's home at The Lakes – by yoo's Design Studio – features a large open-plan living space that opens onto a long timber terrace overlooking the waters of one of the lakes. The H-shaped space includes a kitchen and dining area at one end and a welcoming seating area at the other. Carpeting and rugs subtly delineate the different zones, with a black-and-white rug under the dining table and carpeting within the seating area. A wood-burning fireplace provides a welcoming focal point at this end of the room in a contemporary reinterpretation of the age-old idea of the hearth as a symbol of the home.

Recognizing that this idea still has great resonance, whenever possible yoo tries to include fireplaces in both its apartments and standalone houses, as well as in its communal lounges. 'We love the fireplace,' says Davison. 'Every time we can we will include one – even in warm places like Miami or Singapore. It's more the idea of it than the practical application. A fireplace helps make a home a home and gives warmth in any space. We often have fireplaces in the lobby of a building as well.'

The hearth serves as a reassuring draw in any living space. It's the low-tech antithesis of what has become the other great focal point of many living rooms: the television. Although televisions and other forms of domestic technology have a vital place in the home, it is possible to integrate them with a degree of subtlety, so that they become a discreet presence rather than a dominant element in a room.

'In the Western world the fireplace was always the focus of the sitting room,' says Steve Leung. 'But now not every apartment or a house has a fireplace.

It's wonderful to be able to stretch the eye at home, to have that sense of openness and freedom.

[JH]

In Asia the television is often the focal point. Some people hate it, especially from a Western point of view, where they might not have a television in the sitting room at all. But in Asia ten out of ten sitting rooms will have one. From a designer's point of view you have to ask how to make this look good along with all the other decorative elements. Sometimes we hide them and put the television behind a sliding door so that when the door is closed it may look like a screen or painting, but sometimes it's exposed and becomes part of the room.'

Most importantly, the open-plan layout creates a welcome degree of flexibility within a space. A workstation can easily be introduced, or a play zone for young children in easy view of the rest of the family. This might be enhanced by the use of zoned lighting, which allows different parts of the room to be picked out, creating alternative atmospheres and flavours. Unencumbered by solid partitions and inflexible spaces, the open-plan home can be moulded and adapted to each person's preferences and daily living patterns.

2

**1: At The Jade in New York City, custom-designed boxes hold bathrooms and kitchens but the living spaces remain open-plan.**

**2: In the open-plan living spaces with sea views at Icon Brickell in Miami, a yoo Inspired by Starck design, rugs and wall curtains are subtly used to delineate seating and relaxation zones.**

1

# Kelly Hoppen

**K**elly Hoppen became a designer at the age of sixteen and developed a distinctive 'East meets West' design philosophy that she has set out in her many books. As well as private homes, Hoppen has designed hotels, restaurants, yachts and private jets, while her branded range of products includes furniture, fabrics, paints, wallpapers and home accessories. She is also a television personality and runs her own design school.

**Who were your design heroes when you first started exploring interior design and architecture?**

I didn't really have any. I was sixteen and a half and just passionate about it and started my business then. The only person that I can remember thinking about was David Hicks because his was the very first design book that I got. But I don't think I had any heroes. I went into my own little world and remained there. Hicks was the antithesis to my style but he was such an icon and I was amazed by how nothing in his interiors went together – it was about pattern.

I was more inspired by art and travel and walking in Florence and looking at churches. I prefer going into people's homes and seeing the way they live rather than saying that I was enlightened by the Bauhaus, because that would be lying. Now there are other designers I admire but back then I was young and energetic and just wanted to design in my own style.

**What was your very first design commission and how did it come about?**

It was a kitchen for my stepfather's friend. It was a complete disaster from start to finish, but it was a job. Then I did a really lovely apartment in London for a friend of my brother. From there I got a fantastic job working for a Grand Prix racecar driver and that's really how the business took off.

**To what extent has the progress and growth of your work and business followed a particular plan, or has it evolved organically?**

It's all been organic. I knew I would be successful. I'm an entrepreneur and I have a vision. I know what I want to achieve and I make it happen. Doing my first books and winning the Andrew Martin design award gave me the springboard to really run with it. The business has many facets to it and working for yoo is one part of the business and that came about because John [Hitchcox] is a friend. So everything I have done has come about organically.

**What kind of design projects do you enjoy most and why?**

It's very varied. I only take on work that I enjoy – there's no point otherwise. I am very lucky in that the people who come to me are all extraordinary people from different walks of life. There has to be a synergy; otherwise you can't design.

**What ambitions do you have for the next ten years?**

There's one thing left to do for me, which is to design for film, which I will do eventually. I'm working on a couple of new businesses at the moment. I'm always doing something new, always challenging myself. I would get bored otherwise.

**Do you think your own approach to designing interiors has changed greatly over the past ten years or so and, if so, in what ways?**

It's always evolving. It always goes back to the initial philosophy and nothing in that has changed. A brand that stands its ground and stays at the top has to have strong values and a philosophy that it keeps to. They may evolve but ultimately they are true to their brand. If it works, don't break it.

**1 & 2:** The living room of this house at The Lakes by yoo opens out onto a terrace overlooking the water; its interiors, designed by Kelly Hoppen for yoo, are calm, thoughtful and composed.

**Overleaf:** Rich textures, opulent finishes and statement pieces such as the bookshelves and chandeliers lend a sense of glamour to this apartment at Barkli Virgin House in Moscow, by Kelly Hoppen for yoo.

2

3

**Your interiors are famously calm and relaxing. Has that always been a priority for you in designing a home?**

That has always been there. My underlying approach comes from the East and that's why I am very successful there. My book *East Meets West* was such a phenomenon. In a way I have gone full-circle back to that book, but with a different twist. The 'East meets West' philosophy is still at the heart of what we do.

**When and where are you at your most creative?**

I do need to get away every now and then to recharge, even if it's just for a few days. Not waking up to an alarm; having a free head and observing and seeing and tasting and looking at different things – I'm always aware when I need to do that. The type of design I do is not machine-like. It's much more

creative and instant. It could be done anywhere – anywhere that doesn't have a telephone. Beach, sun, skiing, mountains – anywhere that's different.

**How different is the experience of working on a project for yoo compared to other kinds of commissions and projects?**

It's completely different. It's growing because the demand is there. It's a great format but we don't create machinery – we create couture.

**Do you think that technology will change the home significantly over the next twenty-five years or so?**

Technology is constantly changing and becoming entwined in the way that we live. I'm still very old-fashioned and think that the home is all about luxury and the feel of it. If you have the technology to switch on your lights quicker and make your televisions disappear, that's all well and good, but it doesn't really change the way that the room looks.

**1 & 2: Contrasting textures and calming, subtle colour choices create a relaxed and welcoming environment at Barkli Virgin House.**

**3: In this bedroom suite at Barkli Virgin House, the custom headboard in the bedroom doubles as a screen that partially encloses the dressing area.**

**As a Londoner, how optimistic do you feel about the current British design scene?**

It's fantastic. I'm all for supporting British design and everything that comes out of the country. I think the UK is at the forefront of so much art and design, fashion, music and food. We are miles ahead of everyone else right now and it wasn't like that fifteen years ago. Today we are proud of what we do and definitely not shy about telling everyone. I'm very optimistic about it.

**To what extent do you feel that your design approach to an apartment building or similar development can help build a sense of community and bring people together?**

I know how people want to live. yoo creates the places for people to commune in big developments; my work is to bring a feeling of calmness and harmony to these spaces.

**How much do you think residential developments are now being influenced by the kinds of communal facilities and amenities that used to be more familiar in hotels, clubs and spas?**

I personally prefer to relax on my own, but I can see the value of creating these environments for other people. People may have kids; they may be working and they may want to spend time with other families and have joint gyms and pools and things. I can see it's a really good idea, especially with the stylistic element yoo brings to it.

**Do you feel that there is a greater demand today for opportunities to meet neighbours and bring people together in a more social context, and for carefully thought-out communal spaces, given how anonymous city living can be?**

A lot of people do meet each other like that. What yoo offers is a much more stylish version of a home within a village. It's lovely. It took me years to say hello to my neighbour and the British in particular are quite funny like that, so it's a good thing.

**What other kinds of communal spaces would you like to see in yoo projects in the future?**

A library is nice – the one we created in our Russian project for yoo had lots of books, which is great. People are on computers all the time these days – pick up a book!

**How important is it to provide a dramatic focal point in a private living/sitting room?**

I look at the whole concept of a space rather than one element. From the minute you press the doorbell it has to be an experience; it has to flow, and it has to continue. A lot of design today is about creating a focal point and it fails because your eye is drawn to one thing and then you are disappointed with the rest. Good design is about the whole experience and trying to understand the zoning of the home.

Today we have kitchens that are more beautifully designed than sports cars.

John Hitchcox

This dining area at yoo Pune in India, a yoo Inspired by Starck design, opens onto the surrounding terraces and gardens.

# cook & dine

# cook & dine

*T*he familiar idea that the kitchen is the heart of the home has never been truer. The gradual evolution of open-plan living has put the spotlight firmly on the kitchen, which has become both a key focal point and a design statement in its own right. Little wonder, then, that so much creative attention is now paid to the kitchen, which has become an elegant and carefully crafted showplace as well as a functional hub for the home.

Traditionally, in most Western houses, the kitchen was something to be hidden away. It was a service space, located behind closed doors and treated as a largely functional and practical room. In an era of large household staffs and servants, the kitchen was off-limits for many wealthy families, although the farmhouse kitchen offered a different and more democratic model at the other end of the social spectrum. All began to change in the early 20th century, as households began to shrink and as patterns of living became more relaxed.

By the 1950s and 60s the kitchen was the subject of a great deal of innovation and excitement. A whole new range of time- and space-saving gadgets came on the market, encouraged by a consumer spending boom. The design content and aesthetic appeal of these pieces, from refrigerators to food mixers, became increasingly high as influential designers such as Raymond Loewy applied streamlining techniques not just to trains and cars, but also to household appliances. New materials such as Formica and Linoleum also brought fresh energy to the kitchen, making it a showcase rather than a decorative afterthought.

During the mid-20th century the kitchen therefore began to emerge from the shadows and become an integral part of the home. In Mies van der Rohe's iconic Farnsworth House, built in 1951 in Plano, Illinois, the layout was open-plan and elements such as the kitchen and bathroom were contained in a central service core – a crafted timber box, sitting within the 'universal space', with a galley-style kitchen to one side. This was a hugely influential design and helped to pave the way for the integrated modern kitchen, set neatly within the main living space of a house or apartment. Being so visible, the kitchen had to be crafted and designed with great attention to its aesthetic appeal as well as its functionality.

Many other houses of the period played with semi-open-plan designs in which the kitchen might be partly separated from dining and seating spaces by

**Vibrant splashes of colour, atmospheric lighting and epic views across the city enliven this kitchen and breakfast room at Lodha Fiorenza in Mumbai, designed by Jade Jagger for yoo.**

2

1: A vibrant red dining table
and chairs stand out against the
neutral tones of walls and floors
at Lodha Fiorenza in Mumbai.

2: Dining and seating spaces
naturally coexist in this
apartment at Acqua Iguazu in
Manila, Philippines, designed
by yoo Inspired by Starck.

# Of course kitchens have to look beautiful but they also need to be functional.

[JH]

At Elle Macpherson's house at The Lakes by yoo, in Gloucestershire, UK, designed by yoo Design Studio, the kitchen and dining area sit together at one end of a bright open-plan living space, lifted by touches of colour and pattern.

kitchen counters or storage units, with serving hatches and breakfast bars providing a sense of connection between the two types of space. Whether the layout was fully or only partially open-plan, the kitchen was becoming more visible than ever. Within the more limited dimensions of city apartments the open-plan layout made particular sense, making galley kitchens and other compact designs the staple approaches.

Today, of course, the open-plan kitchen is an intrinsic element of many contemporary homes, and the design content of the kitchen therefore given central consideration in crafting a successful living space. Great thought and attention is given not just to the functionality of the kitchen, but also to the way it is integrated into the space as a whole and to the quality and textures of the materials from which it is made. The kitchen has become a beautifully crafted piece of furniture in and of itself.

The kitchen is even more important on a conceptual level, treated very much as the heart of the home. However intensively the kitchen may be used for cooking and food preparation, it has become one of the most social areas of the home – a multi-functional hub that supports daily routines and entertaining. The kitchen can double as a bar, an eating place or a workstation, and the kitchen island or table is typically the epicentre of day-to-day life in the home, particularly for families.

1

**1:** Cowhide-covered chairs and coloured glassware enliven this dining table at yoo Pune in India, a yoo Inspired by Starck design.

**2:** The kitchen is separated from the dining and seating areas by a countertopped island in this apartment by Kelly Hoppen for yoo at Barkli Virgin House in Moscow.

**Overleaf:** Atmospheric chandelier lighting and sumptuous drapery bring the feel of a high-end restaurant to this communal dining area and bar at Acqua Iguazu.

'The kitchen is everything,' says Philippe Starck. 'The kitchen is a place where people meet – there is activity, there is conversation. It's very important to have a big, open kitchen. For me an apartment is really just a kitchen and bedrooms – that's all.'

Few of us now opt to have a separate formal dining room, meaning that the dining table has come right into the kitchen, or alongside it, as part of the open floorplan. It makes for a much more social space, where a meal can be prepared for friends or family without the cook having to disappear into a separate part of the house. The kitchen table becomes a vital part of the social dynamic of the home, a place for doing homework and catching up on the day, or for sharing time with friends and neighbours.

At Barkli Park in Moscow, a yoo Inspired by Starck project, a large Italianate mirrored dining table sits right at the centre of an open-plan living space, with Murano chandeliers above it. A floating island alongside the table helps to separate the kitchen subtly, as well as providing a serving counter, breakfast bar or extra work surface, while the rest of the kitchen sits within a galley-style design at the back of the room.

At The Jade in New York, Jade Jagger opted for a different spatial approach. Here the apartments were more loft-like in character, and their proportions sometimes modest. The layout of the living space remained open-plan, but the kitchen, utilities and storage are enclosed in a box constructed in the centre of the apartment. The galley kitchen contained within the box can be disguised by folding doors when not in use, while a long dining table stands nearby. The box also serves as a pivotal organizing element in the apartment, helping to separate the master bedroom from the main living space. The bathroom and wardrobes are contained within the reverse face.

'It's like a jewelry box with secret compartments and drawers,' says Mark Davison. 'You can close it all up so that it becomes this unobtrusive, quite discreet object within the space. Those that like it, love it. It doesn't interfere with the living space and never feels dominant.'

Keeping the clutter and mess of cooking and meal preparation from being intrusive is the constant challenge of having an open kitchen. In many yoo projects, especially in Asia and India, there will be two kitchens: an open and

**Left: A custom pod contains the kitchen of this apartment at The Jade in New York City, designed by Jade Jagger for yoo, with folding doors that can be closed to hide any mess from food preparation while dining or relaxing with friends in the open-plan living space.**

**Overleaf: In The Solarium House, designed by yoo Design Studio, at The Lakes by yoo, the open-plan dining area, which sits alongside the kitchen, centres on a rustic timber table, surrounded by benches and top-lit by a pair of sculptural ceiling lights.**

At The Lakes by yoo, a crafted
island with a worktop partially
separates this calming kitchen
from the dining area in an
open-plan living space designed
by Kelly Hoppen for yoo.

sociable kitchen integrated with the open-plan living space, and a rear service
kitchen and utility space that can be used for preparing the messier parts of
a meal and for clearing away plates and cutlery when dining with friends or
family. The idea of front and back kitchens is becoming increasingly familiar
in some parts of the world.

'A statement kitchen that looks good but that is also functional is becoming
more and more important,' says Steve Leung. 'People enjoy cooking for themselves
and for guests. But sometimes in Asia we will have both an Asian kitchen and a
Western kitchen. With Asian cooking there's always a lot of aroma, so sometimes
they prefer to cook those meals in a more enclosed space. But if you are in an
enclosed kitchen it's difficult to share the fun with friends so sometimes there
will also be an open kitchen for more simple kinds of cooking and preparation
– a more social area for people to spend time together. And perhaps you might
have sliding doors between the two kitchens so that they can be closed or open
when appropriate.'

Particular attention is paid to the detailing, quality and finish of these
kitchens, as well as to the technology of the appliances contained within them.
The expectations we have of our kitchens are now extremely high, elevated
by decades of innovation in the design of both kitchens themselves and their
appliances. Homeowners typically take great pleasure and care in deciding
on the finishes, materials and specification of the kitchen.

Having a choice of dining areas, rather than just a single fixed spot in the
home, adds to the sense of flexibility in how living space is used day-to-day.
As well as the dining table itself, and perhaps a breakfast counter in the kitchen,
there can be other options, such as a table and chairs on a balcony or a smaller,
secondary table in the living area that might double as a workstation. In resort
villages, where there is more time and inclination for leisure, the presence of a
range of eating areas – for different kinds of meals and different times of day –
becomes especially important.

Within the wider vertical community, this choice is often taken further with
the provision of bars, restaurants, cafés and breakfast counters in communal
spaces. The social pleasures of eating, dining and drinking together are
important not just to daily life behind the closed doors of the home, but also
serve as welcome adhesives that bind friends and neighbours together.

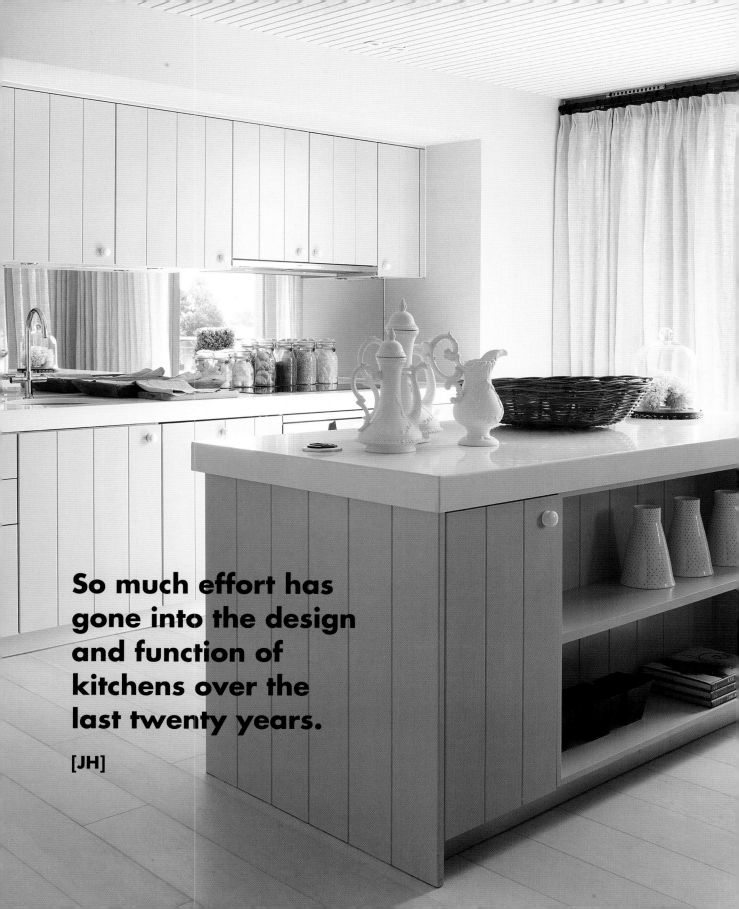

So much effort has gone into the design and function of kitchens over the last twenty years.

[JH]

Steve Leung

*A*rchitect and interior designer Steve Leung is one of the most innovative and successful figures in the world of contemporary Asian design. Born, raised and educated in Hong Kong, Leung founded his own design studio in the city in 1987 and later added four satellite offices across mainland China. His prolific portfolio of work encompasses luxury residential projects, restaurants and hotels, including The Royal Garden, Crowne Plaza Causeway Bay and Hyatt Regency Sha Tin, all in Hong Kong. Leung also designs eponymous ranges of furniture, textiles, wallpapers and home accessories and heads his own restaurant group, 1957 & Co.

**How did you first get involved with architecture and interior design?**

I decided that I wanted to be an architect when I was very young. The reason was that I have an uncle who is an architect. When I was young this uncle lived with us and I used to watch him working at home, doing sketches. He was my idol and a role model in my career.

**Who or what were the biggest influences on your evolution as a designer when you were growing up in Hong Kong?**

I was determined to be an architect from a very young age – less than ten years old. Then I went to the University of Hong Kong to study architecture. So everything seemed to me a smooth experience. Of course, I admired a lot of people when I was studying architecture at university. Le Corbusier was one of my favourite architects at that time. I went to Europe for two months after graduation to visit his projects and his work had a lot of influence on me.

**To what extent is your approach to design and your aesthetic defined by your personal history in Hong Kong and Asia?**

I was born in Hong Kong and I received my education here from primary school all the way through to university. I never left Hong Kong to work or to study. So I always tell people that I am 100% made in Hong Kong. Hong Kong is a very interesting city. Before 1997 it was a British colony, so we are in the middle of two cultures – the Eastern culture and the Western culture. And after 1997 we returned to China, as part of China, and since then I have had a lot of chances to visit and work in China and have become more familiar with its history and culture. So Hong Kong is a very special place. This context has given me a very unique kind of mission and character as far as my design is concerned.

The second thing is my family background. My father had eight brothers and sisters and my father was the eldest son. Although my family was quite well off in my grandfather's day, we were no longer that rich by the time I was born in the 1950s. But our family – especially my grandfather – had a good educational background and was concerned with ethics,

Entrance area of the Sushi
Ta-Ke restaurant in Hong Kong,
designed by Steve Leung.

manners, how you deal with other people. So when I look back, this is something that I really appreciate. There were a lot of expectations on us.

On the other hand, my mother was very modern in her thinking. She was not like the other mothers that I met. She gave me a lot of freedom and let me do whatever I wanted. So I really appreciate the way that my mother treated me. I was quite an independent child when I was growing up.

The third thing is my personal character. Because of my family background I was the kind of child who did a lot of thinking. My mother had no particular guidance on what I needed to do, so from a young age I had to plan my studies, my career – everything. I think I am a very happy person – I always think positively. I am happy almost every day and I am quite easygoing. That is reflected in my design language and the design process and my sense of aesthetics. I want to lead a simple life. I don't want to make it very complicated or do unnecessary things.

**Some people have called you a minimalist, yet many of your hotels and restaurants are very rich in colour, pattern and texture. How would you prefer to define your design philosophy?**

I love and hate the name 'minimalist' that has been given to me. This is not a name I call myself. I am not too offended to be labelled a minimalist, however, because to me minimalism is not actually a design style – it's my philosophy of life; it's an attitude. I always prefer things to be simple, not too pretentious, and not to do things that are unnecessary. I think this is how a minimalist designer should be. But minimalist design for me may be different than minimalist design for you.

When I have to do a casual dining restaurant I do it in a minimalist way. If I have to do a six-star fine-dining hotel restaurant then it has to be more sophisticated. It really depends on the type of work, but regardless of what I am designing, I want to keep my design language right to the

point. Nothing too much. And that's what I understand by minimalism, by my own definition.

**Why do you think that your work has gained the attention of an international audience from Shanghai to London? Do you feel that your aesthetic transcends boundaries and borders especially well?**

I am very fortunate to be living in this period of time, and in such a special place as Hong Kong, which is the doorway to China. It's an international, cosmopolitan city where East meets West and West meets East. Because of my background, I think people will be interested in my work, no matter if it's in Hong Kong, China, London or Europe. With this unique background and during this special period in history, when attention from all over the world is focused on China and Asia, I have the golden opportunity to showcase myself and showcase my work. I'm very lucky to be in Hong Kong and China at this particular point in time.

**As well as Hong Kong, I understand that you also have offices in mainland China. How much potential do you see for your work in Shanghai, Beijing and other major Chinese cities?**

There is huge potential in China. At the moment, aside from our headquarters in Hong Kong, we also have four offices in mainland China, which cover Shanghai, Beijing, Chengdu and Guangzhou – the four major cities in China, at the four corners of the country. It's a huge market. And not only to us – you can see designers and architects in many parts of the world all have opportunities to do good projects in China. Being in Hong Kong, close to China, and where we also speak the same language, is an advantage for us.

**You have designed many hotels, including the Hyatt Hotel in the Sha Tin district of Hong Kong and the Crowne Plaza in Causeway Bay. How difficult is it to come up with an original and engaging design language for a new hotel when the world of international hotel design is now so demanding and competitive?**

It really depends on the project and also on the different hotel operators. Some operators may have a very strong identity. But even with that strong identity, hotel groups all realize that hotels they build in different parts of the world should combine the group's identity with the local culture.

So it's always a mixture, a combination, of the parent company's identity and the local culture. The question is only how much – what percentage of each to get the right balance. Some hotel groups tend to accept a lot of innovation when they go into some very interesting cities. In China, for instance, some of the cities have very strong local cultures. Hong Kong is more metropolitan but if you go to some of the old cities in China the design will be very different. It's always a blend of the local culture and history with the international design philosophy of the hotel.

**To what extent have you seen the kind of luxury amenities that you would traditionally design for a hotel – spas, swimming pools, gyms, libraries, communal lounges and bars – appearing in residential developments?**

This is a very special situation for luxurious residential developments in Asia and particularly for those in Hong Kong and China. We all know that property prices in Hong Kong and some parts of China are really high, so to convince people to buy residences at such a high premium developers definitely need to provide amenities. This is something quite unique. It really happens a lot in Hong Kong and China where the amenities are becoming more luxurious and comprehensive.

But it also depends on the scale of the development. If it's a sizeable residential development at a luxury level then they will provide indoor–outdoor swimming pools, a spa, a clubhouse that will consist of a gymnasium and a library – a lot of different things, even a party room. This is very common in Asia and something that you must have in luxurious developments.

**I understand that as well as designing restaurants, you own three of your own in Hong Kong. Do you enjoy being a restaurateur?**

I actually own four restaurants now. I have two Thai restaurants, called Mango Tree, then I have a Japanese sushi restaurant and an Italian restaurant called Bella Vita. The first reason that I wanted to go into the restaurant business was because I enjoy eating very much, so I love to have my own restaurant where I can enjoy myself and entertain guests.

The second reason is that I have been designing so many restaurants for the last twenty years and whenever I finish my work and look back I never think that the restaurant is perfect. So I wanted to design a restaurant where everything is under my control and create everything from a design point of view. I don't mean just interior design, but the lighting, the menus, the staff uniforms, from the smallest detail to the entire interior ambience. Then I hope the restaurant can be close to perfect – although of course a restaurant can never really be completely perfect.

I really enjoy being a restaurateur. The reason why I can make this into a reality is because I have two very good partners. One is Tino Kwan, an excellent lighting designer who loves food and can cook very well. The other is Paul Kwok, who is one of my clients. He's from Hong Kong, but left in his mid-twenties and moved to Singapore and then went to the Middle East. While he was there he came back to Hong Kong to look for someone to design a restaurant for him in Dubai. He came to me and we worked very well together. So when I had the idea of opening my own restaurant I asked him if he would be interested in coming back to Hong Kong to work with me and my partner to start a restaurant business. Paul knows the business inside out. Without him I'd have no ability to operate and open my own restaurants. So it's a very good combination. The three of us work together very happily and we have the same goals.

**Do you think that you will open other restaurants in the future and perhaps a hotel of your own one day?**

We have four restaurants already and are just opening another Japanese restaurant and a Vietnamese restaurant, also in Hong Kong. We want to open one or two restaurants every year and one of my greatest aims is to open a Chinese restaurant. Cantonese is my favourite cuisine. I'd like to open a Chinese restaurant – maybe in Hong Kong, maybe in China, maybe in Europe. This is my dream. I want to do it in the near future.

My ultimate dream is to open a hotel of my own. It would definitely not be a hotel with 500 rooms. It would be a boutique hotel of perhaps ten to fifteen rooms and certainly not more than fifty. It's my dream project. It might be in Hong Kong, China, or another part of the world. I really can't tell you exactly where at this moment, but this is one of my ultimate aims.

**Would you say that travelling in Japan, Europe and other parts of the world has influenced your work?**

Japan is a place that I love to go – it's a very interesting country and also relatively close to Hong Kong. Japan and Europe are the two places where I spend a good deal of time when I go on holidays and travel. It has been an influence on my work because I spend a lot of time looking at different things while I am travelling, both in Japan and Europe. Normally I will come to Europe at least twice a year, sometimes more than that – Italy, France, London. I get inspiration from whatever I have seen.

**What are you looking forward to most about working with John Hitchcox and yoo in the coming years?**

John Hitchcox and I come from very different backgrounds. Being somebody from the East, based in Hong Kong and having an Asian background, I think that in working with John Hitchcox this combination of cultures will be a very good starting point for doing something different. yoo has several different creative directors and all of them come from the West, especially Europe. So I'm the first Asian designer to be invited to join yoo as a creative director and hopefully this will create something very interesting.

With yoo there may also be more opportunities to work overseas – in Europe, the Middle East, Russia or South America – places where yoo has a lot of influence. But at the same time I want to help bring yoo to Asia through my connections here, both in Hong Kong and in other parts of Asia. So it's a very interesting chemistry.

# Bathrooms and bedrooms are secrets but they should be places of great beauty and attraction.

**John Hitchcox**

A relaxed bedroom, including space for a seating area, decorated in the 'Minimal' palette by yoo Inspired by Starck at Acqua Iguazu, Manila, Philippines.

# bathing & indulging

# bathing & indulging

*T*he modern home has many different roles and functions. It is a place of communication and interaction; a place to cook, dine and entertain. Our homes may also be our places of work as well as venues for leisure, recreation and relaxation. Above all, however, a home is a personal sanctuary where we can retreat from the pace and pressures of the world beyond its walls and enjoy the freedom of being in our own chosen haven.

Vertical villages in bustling city centres have a particular resonance when we speak of the idea of the home as a retreat. Urban living in thriving cities has much to recommend it, with countless cultural, social and intellectual activities constantly on offer, as well as centres of business and exchange. But it is always important to be able to step across the threshold of our own building, entering our private territory and savouring the sense of wellbeing and belonging. The vertical village itself offers many different opportunities to socialize with our neighbours, friends and family in the enticing communal spaces that add such richness to daily life; however, there will always come a time when we want to retreat further behind closed doors.

Philippe Starck sees two essential realms within the home. There is the more 'public' realm that includes the kitchen, sitting area and dining places. Then there is the 'private' realm – the bedroom and the bathroom. Here, especially, we want to be able to relax, unwind and to indulge ourselves in comfort and ease. These are the places to be ourselves, to decompress. Just because these spaces are personal and more hidden, however, no less attention is given to their planning and design. They are always treated as vital and special parts of the home.

The bedroom has become an increasingly indulgent and important space. Partly influenced by the design of hotel rooms, bedrooms are no longer simply nighttime cocoons. Luxurious bedrooms have enough room for seating areas, which may serve as evening lounges or places to read, watch television, talk and listen to music away from the more open and expansive living spaces of the apartment.

Within yoo Berlin, a yoo Inspired by Starck project, the bedrooms are generously scaled with room enough for a seating area. A vast Venetian mirror against one wall reinforces the sense of space and scale, while statement lighting brings glamour and personality to the room. Similarly, at the Sans Souci in Vienna, designed by yoo Studio, a large mirror along one wall is a key element, along with a four-poster bed and a bank of integrated wardrobes fronted with bespoke golden doors.

**A striking bathroom with an Art Deco flavour at the Sans Souci Hotel & Residences, Vienna, by yoo Studio.**

# The idea of a bathroom as another sitting room or lounge is rather wonderful.

[JH]

At the Sans Souci Hotel & Residences, a four-poster bed sits at the centre of this warm, enticing space, with an elegant sequence of golden wardrobes to the rear.

**Overleaf:**
p. 184: A children's bedroom with bunk beds and space to play at Lodha Fiorenza in Mumbai, designed by Jade Jagger for yoo.

p. 185: Honey-coloured mosaic tiles and twin sinks bring an elegant graphic aesthetic to this bathroom at Icon Vallarta in Puerto Vallarta, Mexico, a yoo Inspired by Starck design.

When space allows, a dressing room is also a welcome addition. 'I love a dressing room,' says Jade Jagger. 'One of the ultimate luxuries is to have a dressing room and a big bathroom. They are things that enhance the daily routine of life so that the rituals of bathing and dressing become real pleasures.'

At Jagger for yoo's Lodha Fiorenza in Mumbai, bedrooms and bathrooms are rich in character and texture. Peacock-feather marquetry enhances the custom timber headboard in the bedroom and forms a framework for wardrobes and the makeup table in the dressing area. Mosaic tilework and his-and-hers sink units alongside generously scaled bathtubs make the bathrooms equally welcoming.

Children's bedrooms, too, are given a great deal of thought. Jagger has designed rooms at Lodha Fiorenza that are playful and engaging, with space for bunk beds, a reading chair and play area, recognizing that children's rooms are increasingly multi-functional micro-worlds, studio apartments in miniature. At yoo Pune, an Inspired by Starck project, also in India, there is again space enough for seating and play areas in the children's bedrooms, which are decorated with vibrant wallpapers whose splashes of colour enliven an otherwise neutral palette for floors and walls. Bunk beds also feature at The Lakes by yoo, in the English Cotswolds, where they bring a more social aspect to children's bedrooms, making it possible for siblings and friends to share the same room during the holidays or have sleepover parties.

Bedroom and bathroom spaces within a suite are becoming increasingly integrated and the relationship between the two is more fluid than ever.

1

**1:** Lavender-coloured tiles create striking contrast in a shower room at Elle Macpherson's house, by yoo Design Studio, at The Lakes by yoo in Gloucestershire, UK.

**2:** A Piero Fornasetti wallpaper provides an engaging and playful backdrop to this bedroom at yoo Pune in India, a yoo Inspired by Starck project, with room for a chaise longue and a desk as well as a four-poster bed.

**Overleaf:** A generously scaled tub dominates this bathroom at The Solarium House, by yoo Design Studio, at The Lakes by yoo, while the oversized vase adds an unexpected and playful touch.

**The bathroom is an opportunity
to create something beautiful
that is quite personal to you.**

[JH]

In some of the most cutting-edge home designs the boundaries between bedroom and bathroom are beginning to dissolve altogether. In a house designed by Kelly Hoppen for yoo at The Lakes, for instance, the two can either be opened up to form a single room or divided by a sliding door.

The bathroom has become a carefully crafted entity in itself, mirroring the evolution of the kitchen from functional service space to thoughtfully designed showpiece, combining practicality and beauty. 'When people first started to have bathrooms they thought they should be like a machine – a machine for washing,' says Philippe Starck. 'But it doesn't need to look like a machine – it can look like a salon. You can put whatever you want on the walls or on the floor. I have designed many bathroom furnishings that can stand alone, like a sofa or an armchair. And after that you can bring in any type of table, a fireplace, a lamp and it's still a bathroom.

'People think that a bathroom has to be a perfect box made of tiles, with everything like a spacelab, but it's not true. We don't need to live in a spacelab because we're not in space. Take any room and put in a bathtub and a shower and a sink and it's a bathroom.'

Starck has much experience in designing products for the bathroom, including baths, sinks and more for Duravit, as well as taps and shower systems for Hansgrohe. The choice of designer products for the bathroom has expanded greatly in recent years, and many of these pieces are shaped with a lightness of touch that plays down their mechanical aspects and makes it possible to use them in the more visible areas of the home. Baths become sculptures floating in space; a shower head becomes a shining spout emerging from a beautifully finished wall or ceiling.

**Wall tiles arranged in a geometric formation and a crafted vanity–sink unit with patterned timber panels offer much to engage the eye in this bathroom at Lodha Fiorenza.**

# It's important to make bathrooms that are both cosy and sensual.

[JH]

At this house designed by Kelly Hoppen for yoo at The Lakes by yoo, a sliding timber door can be used to separate bedroom and bathroom, if desired.

Starck, like Wanders and yoo's own design studio, also has extensive experience in hotel and spa design, both of which influence the aesthetic and ambience of domestic bathrooms as they become ever more luxurious and deserving of attention, featuring fine materials, organic textures and a highly creative approach to design. More space is now devoted to the bathroom than ever, with walk-in showers, generous bathtubs, vanity units, and – increasingly – even fireplaces and sofas. The bathroom is now seen as a place in which one wants to spend time, emulating the hotel and spa experience. It is a key room in the house for unwinding and relaxing, either alone or with your partner. If both time and space are the ultimate luxuries, the prospect of an hour spent in a welcoming, well-proportioned bathroom – perhaps with a fire roaring on the hearth and a good book to hand – becomes powerfully attractive.

The bathrooms at yoo Istanbul, a yoo Inspired by Starck building, are generously proportioned, with high ceilings. A large bathtub sits in one corner, surrounded by candles, while flowers are displayed in a niche set into the smooth, plastered walls. The circular bathrooms of the Sans Souci in Vienna have an opulent quality, with high, domed ceilings, atmospheric lighting and marble floors. The level of detailing, thought and quality materials invested in these spaces makes them key elements of the home rather than functional afterthoughts.

Although cultural differences affect the specific bathroom elements and fixtures that are used in individual developments around the world, the attention paid to the design and specification of these most intimate and personal of spaces is now universal. This is especially true in Asia, where designers such as Steve Leung focus particular attention on the bathroom.

'Everybody is working hard – particularly in China and Hong Kong – and everybody spends a lot of time working and in the office,' says Leung. 'So when they get back home the places where they spend the most time are the bedroom and bathroom. So the bathroom is very important. People want a very comfortable and functional bathroom. Although it may be a small bathroom with just a shower, a vanity unit and counter, there will be marble or other natural stone on the walls and floors, and the highest quality fittings. Sometimes there may be a concealed television, underfloor heating or integrated music. So even in quite a small space the functions will be very comprehensive.'

Together the bedroom and bathroom represent a haven within the home – an inner sanctum for peaceful enjoyment and pure escapism. These are spaces where you can be at your most relaxed, your most thoughtful or your most open and vulnerable. More than any other space in the home, they must therefore offer comfort and character suited to your temperament and mood.

**Opposite:** This vibrant orange armchair provides the perfect counterfoil to the crisp, sophisticated luxury of the marble and glass shower in a bathroom at yoo Pune.

**Overleaf:** Bunk beds save space and bring a sense of fun to this children's bedroom, complete with a rocking sofa for story time, at The Solarium House designed by yoo Design Studio at The Lakes by yoo.

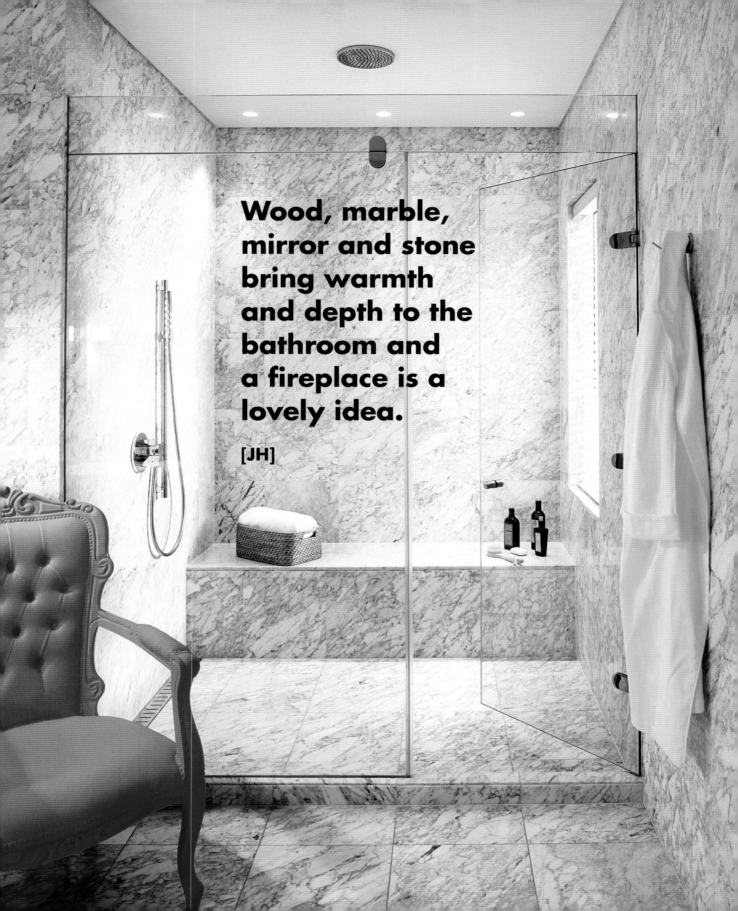

**Wood, marble, mirror and stone bring warmth and depth to the bathroom and a fireplace is a lovely idea.**

[JH]

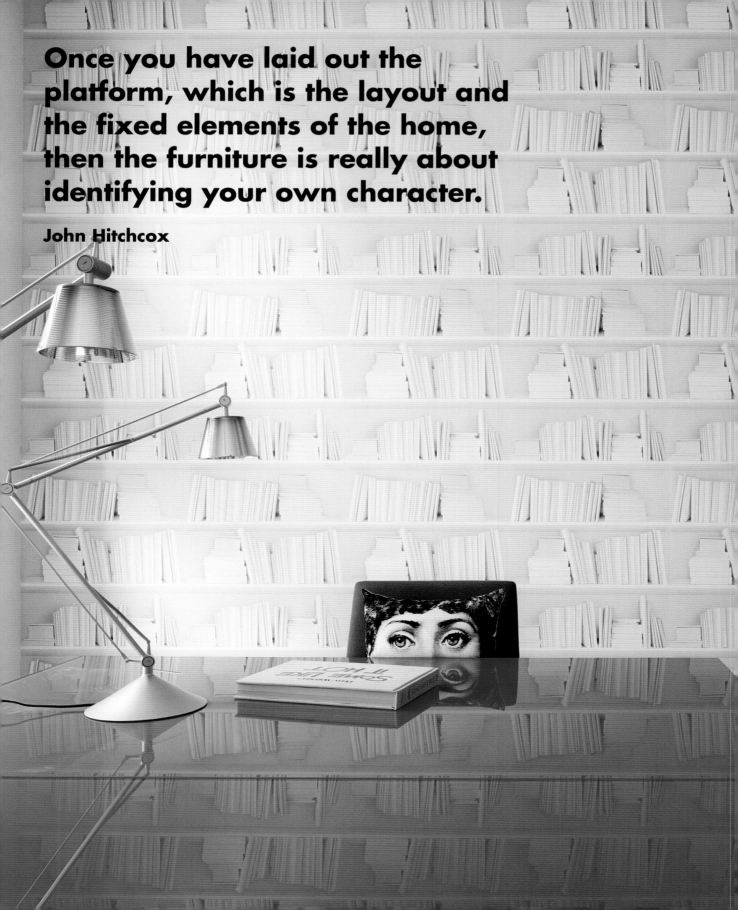

**Once you have laid out the platform, which is the layout and the fixed elements of the home, then the furniture is really about identifying your own character.**

John Hitchcox

The bookcase wallpaper, standing library rack, red table and Piero Fornasetti cushion create an engaging composition in this study zone at Barkli Park in Moscow, a yoo Inspired by Starck design.

# finishing touches

# finishing touches

**H**owever well-designed the vertical village, however generously equipped with indoor and outdoor communal spaces, inspiring kitchens, and luxurious bathing and sleeping areas, it is the personal, finishing touches that truly make an apartment feel like your own home, an oasis of individuality within the anonymity of a large city.

Fluid, open-plan living spaces provide flexible frameworks that can support an infinite range of interiors, but input from the homeowner is the essential ingredient in creating a stylish, welcoming and deeply human urban home. In selecting flooring, fittings, furniture, drapery, carpets, art and other decorations, whether alone or assisted by professionals, each resident helps to craft an urban living space that reflects his or her own lifestyle and aesthetic tastes. The old image of the high-rise apartment as a sterile, anonymous, mass-produced cube has been decisively banished to history.

yoo's house of designers, along with its own studio, have developed a range of 'palettes' that provide many different opportunities to introduce individual character and personality into the home. Each designer brings a distinctive aesthetic approach and a deep-rooted understanding of every aspect of crafting interior space. When Philippe Starck, Marcel Wanders, Jade Jagger, Kelly Hoppen or Steve Leung put their name to a yoo building, they work with yoo's design studio in both creating enticing communal spaces and refining the interiors palettes available for each home. These palettes – which cover every fixed element, including kitchens and bathrooms – give clients the chance to select from a tailored menu of materials, finishes and aesthetic styles. It is in effect an interiors service authored by the leading names in the world of design.

'We help people to know themselves,' says Starck, 'and to recognize their own style. Once they have chosen their style, we can determine all the basics, such as the floors, countertops, door handles. For instance, if you like the "Nature" palette, you will probably like a plain wood floor, natural limestone tops, and a specific type of handles. With the palettes we know that people will be better equipped to make their own home the way that they like.'

Starck's 'Nature' palette draws inspiration from the natural world, with materials such as oak, limestone and marble. The 'Culture' palette is rich, sophisticated and eclectic, blending influences from history, art and travel. The 'Minimal' palette places an emphasis on simplicity with a clean, calm aesthetic, yet one still full of texture and warmth. The fourth Starck palette, 'Classic', is about timeless craftsmanship and excellence in detailing and finish, using sensual materials and earthy, warm colours.

**Opposite: Strong and engaging photographic images add an additional, flexible dimension to a space, as seen here in a library corner at Icon Brickell in Miami, a yoo Inspired by Starck design.**

**Overleaf: Peacock motifs are repeated in both decorative photography on the wall and the intricate panelling of the wooden headboard in a bedroom by Jade Jagger for yoo at Lodha Fiorenza in Mumbai.**

Each member of the yoo family has designed a distinctive series of palettes that best express his or her own aesthetic approach while presenting a wide variety of options to each homeowner. For Marcel Wanders the palettes are 'Eclectic', 'New Antiques', 'Natural' and 'Architectural.' 'Techno', 'Club', 'Disco' and 'Boho' form the Jade Jagger options (see p. 115). Kelly Hoppen and Steve Leung have created their own design styles as well. yoo's design studio collaborates on the delivery of all these palettes, while also developing additional design options of its own.

'Within each style all of the bathrooms are different, the light fittings, the floor finishes,' says Mark Davison, the head of yoo's design studio. 'It's about creating a stage for living with fabulously beautiful materials, so you can't really go wrong. You've set the stage with these elements and then the real drama, the character, comes through with the furniture.'

Furnishing the apartment also involves a wide degree of choice. It may be a matter of shaping the home with your own individual selection of furniture, an idea that Starck, especially, encourages as part of the process of bringing your own personality to a space. But there is also the option to select furniture from yoo's own suggested range of pieces, which includes exclusive yoo designs and pieces created by Starck, Wanders, Hoppen and other members of the design family.

'We can offer furniture suggestions or packages. Sometimes people want a turn-key solution with fully furnished apartments and we can do that too,' says Davison. 'But we really started with the idea of helping people to make a home of their own. Our aim is that the end-user can make those choices themselves and bring in whatever they want.'

There may be a temptation to choose pieces by yoo designers, partly because the furniture created by members of the collective has such wide resonance in the world of design as a whole and integrates so well into contemporary interiors. Starck's line of furniture includes modern icons such as the Louis Ghost and Dr No chairs for Kartell, as well as his Bubble Club armchairs and sofas for outdoor use. There are also Starck pieces available from Driade, Cassina, Magis and other firms. Starck's lighting is produced by Flos, Dedon and Baccarat with key designs including his giant anglepoise

**A Piero Fornasetti lamp adds wit and interest to this seating area in a lounge at yoo Pune in India, designed by yoo Inspired by Starck.**

**The most important thing is to identify what makes you feel comfortable and then build slowly. Don't rush – you don't have to finish an entire home overnight.**

[JH]

# Try not to make it too minimal – make it warm, make it personal, make it evocative.

[JH]

**Right:** Geometric wallpaper, deep-pile wool carpeting, textured rugs and stools add plenty of visual interest and tactile pleasure to this playroom at The Solarium House, by yoo Design Studio, at The Lakes by yoo, in Gloucestershire, UK.

**Overleaf:**
**p. 208:** Single roses arranged in a collection of glass vases add vibrancy to this tablescape at yoo Istanbul, designed by yoo Inspired by Starck.

**p. 209:** Limited splashes and highlights of bold colour can bring a real sense of dynamic energy to a space without being overwhelming, as in this seating corner at yoo Pune.

Superarchimoon lamp from Flos. Marcel Wanders, too, is the author of many modern, characterful lighting and furniture designs, including pieces produced by Moooi, the design house that he co-founded in 2001 and for which he serves as artistic director, as well as running his own design studio. Some of Wanders's most famous pieces include his Skygarden and Zeppelin ceiling lights for Flos, along with his iconic Knotted Chair of 1996 for Cappellini. Kelly Hoppen and Steve Leung also have their own ranges of furniture, textiles and other decorative pieces: Hoppen's include a kitchen collection with Smallbone and a wallpaper range with Graham & Brown; Leung has created furniture for Maxxa and Actus.

Expressing personal eclecticism and individual character is especially important in decorating an urban home, given the sometimes impersonal nature of life in a metropolis. This means that furniture and lighting are mixed and matched according to individual taste, and to respond to the atmosphere of individual spaces. Antique and vintage pieces are welcome additions to the mix. Mid-century classics by Charles and Ray Eames, Eero Saarinen, George Nelson and others introduce a reassuringly familiar, yet sophisticated, note to interiors, alongside the highly sculptural and organic nature of work by Alvar Aalto and Hans Wegner. Such mid-century modernist pieces sit easily within contemporary interiors and often appear in spaces that feature a successful blend of vintage and new.

There should always be the opportunity to add a third and final layering of character to the home, beyond its fixed elements and furniture. This is the more

**1:** A world map on the ceiling adds a new dimension to this relaxing space at Acqua Iguazu, Manila, Philippines, designed by yoo Inspired by Starck.

**2:** Art, texture and graphic interest (courtesy of a Piero Fornasetti wallpaper) combine in an original way at yoo Pune.

**Overleaf:** An overscaled lime green anglepoise lamp by Philippe Starck introduces a playful note and a spark of colour to this reflective room at The Lakes by yoo.

2

1

**Opposite:** Personal items such as ceramics and throws add another aesthetic layer to the home, as seen here at yoo Pune.

**Overleaf:**
**p. 216:** This sculptural table at yoo Pune is a statement piece in and of itself while the bell-jar artwork adds a fresh, personal dimension.

**p. 217:** A warm wallpaper pattern with a forest motif is echoed by the tree-trunk side tables in this bedroom at Acqua Iguazu.

personal selection of art, ceramics and glass as well as soft furnishings such as cushions, throws and fabrics, and the books and other valued treasures that help make a space one's own. 'It's about the art pieces, some of the accessories, the artefacts, the table settings,' says Leung. 'All these things help bring character and identity to an apartment that reflects the taste and style of the owner.'

Key to this concept of choice is the idea that ultimately a space should truly reflect the taste and style of the owner. The process of achieving this may be made easier and more enjoyable for the client through being able to draw upon the talents of leading professional designers. But the finishing touches and the distinctive personality expressed within a space are always down to the individual. The strong bones and fluid, open architecture of a well-designed apartment allow daily choices about how one lives within a space, as well as the freedom and flexibility to move pieces around and update a room.

In many ways, this idea of choice underpins the whole concept of the vertical village. The village offers daily choices within the broader definition of home, which encompasses communal lounges, spas, pools and gyms. These options allow each resident to shape their own daily and weekly routines, with opportunities not just for fitness and leisure, but also for sharing valuable time with partners, family and friends.

The vertical village, then, offers an astonishing level of freedom and choice right at the heart of the city. Each resident plays a part in shaping not just the individual identity of their own private space but also the overall atmosphere and dynamics of their own community. In this way the anonymity and sterility that can sometimes blight city living is banished in the vertical village and the high-rise home, now more than ever, is a place of enjoyment, exchange and delight.

Allow change and allow your space to breathe. Feel free to move things around, which is the beauty of an open plan.

[JH]

# PROJECT DIRECTORY

Note: page numbers in *italic* refer to images. Details of projects that were in the early stages of development at the time of printing may be subject to change without notice.

## Argentina

### yoo Nordelta
City: Buenos Aires
Neighbourhood: Nordelta Tigre
Developer: K Group
Designer: yoo Inspired by Starck
Units: 470
See pages: *24–25, 62–63, 72–73, 76–77, 97, 101, 102–3, 104*

## Australia

### Tribeca
City: Melbourne
Neighbourhood: East Melbourne
Developer: R Corporation
Designer: yoo Inspired by Starck
Units: 440

### yoo Meta
City: Sydney
Neighbourhood: Surry Hills
Developer: Carrington Group
Designer: yoo Inspired by Starck
Units: 83

## Austria

### Sans Souci Hotel & Residences
City: Vienna
Neighbourhood: Spittelberg

Developer: Sans Souci
Designer: yoo Studio
Units: 15 residences + 65 hotel room
See pages: *22–23, 25, 180*, 181, *182–183*, 194

## Canada

### seventy5Portland
City: Toronto
Neighbourhood: King West
Developer: Freed Developments
Designer: yoo Inspired by Starck
Units: 232
See pages: *34*

### yooMontreal
City: Montreal
Neighbourhood: Delson
Developer: Le Constructions Chapam Inc
Designer: yoo Inspired by Starck
Units: 100

## China

### J Plus (formerly JIA Hotel)
City: Hong Kong
Neighbourhood: Causeway Bay
Developer: PC Asia
Designer: yoo Inspired by Starck
Units: 70

### Mira Moon
City: Hong Kong
Neighbourhood: Wanchai
Developer: Henderson Group operated by Miramar
Designer: Wanders & yoo

Units: 91
See pages: *18–19, 33, 83, 86*

### yoo Residence
City: Hong Kong
Neighbourhood: Causeway Bay
Developer: Couture Homes
Designer: yoo Studio
Units: 138

## Germany

### yoo Berlin
City: Berlin
Neighbourhood: Berlin-Mitte
Developer: Peach Property Group
Designer: yoo Inspired by Starck
Units: 86
See pages: *126–27, 132–33*, 181

### yoo Hamburg
City: Hamburg
Neighbourhood: HafenCity
Developer: Vivacon
Designer: yoo Inspired by Starck
Units: 60

### yoo Munich
City: Munich
Neighbourhood: Glockenbach Quarter
Developer: Vivacon
Designer: yoo Inspired by Starck
Units: 69

## India

### Lodha Evoq
City: Mumbai

Neighbourhood: Wadala
Developer: Lodha Group
Designer: yoo Inspired by Starck
Units: 340
See pages: *4, 126, 131, 135*

**Lodha Fiorenza**
City: Mumbai
Neighbourhood: Goregaon
Developer: Lodha Group
Designer: Jade Jagger for yoo
Units: 200
See pages: *34–35, 60, 106–7, 118, 119, 152, 154, 184, 186, 190–91, 202–3*

**Karma Lakelands**
City: New Delhi
Neighbourhood: Gurgaon
Developer: Unitech
Designer: yoo Inspired by Starck
Units: 448

**Water's Edge**
City: Bangalore
Neighbourhood: Nagavara
Developer: Equinox
Designer: Jade Jagger for yoo
Units: 80

**Kelly Hoppen for yoo Villas**
City: Pune
Neighbourhood: Wagholi
Developer: Wagholi Properties
    Private Limited
Designer: Kelly Hoppen for yoo

**yoo Pune**
City: Pune

Neighbourhood: Koregaon Park Annexe
Developer: Panchshil
Designer: yoo Inspired by Starck
Units: 228
See pages: *11, 17, 42–43, 52, 53, 104, 120–21, 150–51, 158, 186, 186–87, 195, 205, 209, 211, 215, 216*

## Indonesia

**LePang**
City: Jakarta
Neighbourhood: South Jakarta
Developer: PT Dalawa Paralia Lepang
Designer: Jade Jagger for yoo
Units: 80 + 40

**Peruri88**
City: Jakarta
Neighbourhood: South Jakarta
Developer: PT Benhil Property
Designer: yoo Studio

**Postmark, yoo2 Hotel**
City: Jakarta
Neighbourhood: South Jakarta
Developer: Epimeinoume Investindo
Designer: Jade Jagger for yoo

## Israel

**yoo Tel Aviv**
City: Tel Aviv
Neighbourhood: Ramat Aviv
Developer: Habas Group
Designer: yoo Inspired by Starck
Units: 150 + 150

## Mexico

**Icon Vallarta**
City: Puerto Vallarta
Neighbourhood: Bahía de Banderas
Developer: The Related Group
Designer: yoo Inspired by Starck
Units: 343
See pages: *54–55, 58–59, 65, 75, 78–79, 90–91, 95, 185*

## Panama

**yoo Panama**
City: Panama City
Neighbourhood: Balboa Avenue
Developer: Habitat
Designer: yoo Inspired by Starck
Units: 203
See pages: *12, 69, 70*

## Peru

**Malecon**
City: Lima
Neighbourhood: Miraflores
Developer: ACM Grupo
Designer: yoo Inspired by Starck
Units: 32

## Philippines

**Aqua Boracay**
City: Boracay Island
Neighbourhood: Bulabog Beach
Developer: Acqua Boracay Group
Designer: yoo Studio
Units: 134
See pages: *20–21*

*142, 143, 156–57, 164–65, 167, 186, 186, 188–89, 192–93, 196–97, 206–7, 212–13*

### NW8
City: London
Neighbourhood: St John's Wood
Developer: yoo
Designer: yoo Inspired by Starck
Units: 38

### Vauxhall Skygardens
City: London
Neighbourhood: Vauxhall
Developer: Frasers Project Limited
Designer: yoo Studio

## Uruguay

### yoo Punta del Este
City: Punta del Este
Neighbourhood: Art District
Developer: K Group
Designer: yoo Inspired by Starck
Units: 250

## USA

### Downtown
City: New York
Neighbourhood: Financial District, off Wall Street
Developer: Boymelgreen
Designer: yoo Inspired by Starck
Units: 326
See pages: *10, 14–15, 69, 92, 101, 129*

### Dwell95
City: New York

Neighbourhood: Wall Street
Developer: Moinian
Designer: yoo Inspired by Starck
Units: 507
See pages: *30, 44, 45, 50, 51, 70, 70–71*

### Echo Brickell
City: Miami
Neighbourhood: Brickell Corridor
Developer: PMG Brickell, LLC
Designer: yoo Studio
Units: 158

### The Gramercy
City: New York
Neighbourhood: Gramercy Park
Developer: Victor Homes
Designer: yoo Inspired by Starck
Units: 200
See pages: *56*

### Icon Brickell
City: Miami
Neighbourhood: Brickell
Developer: The Related Group
Designer: yoo Inspired by Starck
Units: 1,855
See pages: *20, 26–27, 39, 40, 41, 74, 78, 104–5, 109, 139, 200*

### Icon South Beach
City: Miami
Neighbourhood: South Beach
Developer: The Related Group
Designer: yoo Inspired by Starck
Units: 289
See pages: *38–39, 39, 46–47*

### Parris Landing
City: Boston
Neighbourhood: Charleston Navy Yard
Developer: Carlyle Group
Designer: yoo Inspired by Starck
Units: 367

### The Jade
City: New York
Neighbourhood: Flatiron District
Developer: Copper Group
Designer: Jade Jagger for yoo
Units: 57
See pages: *8–9, 32, 98–99, 101, 114, 115, 116–17, 124–25, 138–39, 162, 162–63, 163*

### yooD4
City: Boston
Neighbourhood: South End
Developer: Urbanica
Designer: yoo Inspired by Starck
Units: 26

### yoo Metropica
City: Atlanta
Neighbourhood: Midtown
Developer: Metropica Residential I, LLC
Designer: yoo Studio

### yoo on the Park
City: Atlanta
Neighbourhood: Midtown
Developer: Tivoli
Designer: yoo Inspired by Starck
Units: 249

# AUTHOR BIOGRAPHIES
# & ACKNOWLEDGMENTS

**Dominic Bradbury** is a design writer and freelance journalist who contributes to many magazines and newspapers around the world, including *The Telegraph*, the *Financial Times*, *House & Garden* and *World of Interiors*. His many books include *Mediterranean Modern*, *New Natural Home*, *The Iconic House* and *The Iconic Interior*, all published by Thames & Hudson. He lives in Norfolk.

Dominic would like to thank all at yoo for their support and valued assistance, particularly co-author John Hitchcox, as well as Mark Davison, Michelle van Vuuren, Hannah Godwin and Anna Rowlands. Special thanks are also due to Philippe Starck, Marcel Wanders, Steve Leung, Jade Jagger, Tom Bartlett and Kelly Hoppen. He would also like to express his gratitude to the team at Thames & Hudson, designer Peter Dawson at Grade Design, and photographer Mel Yates.

**John Hitchcox** is one of Europe's most innovative design-based property developers. As co-founder of the Manhattan Loft Corporation, he is credited with establishing New York-style loft living in London. A renowned pioneer of design-led development, John founded yoo in collaboration with Philippe Starck in 1999. The company now has developments in some thirty countries worldwide and is recognized as the largest residential property brand in the world.

John would like to thank a number of people for their collaboration and support in the writing of this book. First and foremost my very great thanks goes to Dominic Bradbury and to all the creative directors at yoo; and to Philippe Starck, Jade Jagger, Marcel Wanders, Kelly Hoppen, Tom Bartlett and Steve Leung. A special thank you also goes to Michelle van Vuuren and our wonderful team at yoo.

# IMAGE CREDITS

2, 3, 4 CGI; 6 Courtesy of yoo;  8–9, 10 Paul Rivera; 11 Francis Amiand; 12 Claudia Uribe; 14 Paul Rivera; 15 Mel Yates; 17 Francis Amiand; 18, 20 CGI; 21 Miguel Nacianceno; 22–23 CGI; 24 Eugenio Valentini; 25 Gregor Titze; 26–27 Claudia Uribe; 28–29 CGI; 30, 32 Paul Rivera; 33, 34 CGI; 35 Mel Yates; 36–37 CGI; 38–39, 40, 41 Claudia Uribe; 42–43 Francis Amiand; 45 Paul Rivera; 46–47 Claudia Uribe; 48 Nicolas Guerin; 50–51 Paul Rivera; 52–53 Francis Amiand; 54–55 Claudia Uribe; 56 Paul Rivera; 58–59 Claudia Uribe; 60 Mel Yates; 62–63 CGI; 65 Claudia Uribe; 66–67 Courtesy of Marcel Wanders Studio; 68 CGI; 69 Courtesy of Marcel Wanders Studio; 70–71 Paul Rivera; 72–73 CGI; 74–75 Claudia Uribe; 76–77 CGI; 78–79 Claudia Uribe; 80 Courtesy of Marcel Wanders Studio; 83 CGI; 84–85 Courtesy of Marcel Wanders Studio; 86 CGI; 88–89 Courtesy of Marcel Wanders Studio; 90–91 Claudia Uribe; 92 Paul Rivera; 94 Mel Yates; 95 Claudia Uribe; 97 Eugenio Valentini; 98–99 Paul Rivera; 100 Mel Yates; 101, 102–103 Eugenio Valentini; 104 CGI; 105 Paul Rivera; 106–7, 108–9, 110, 112–13 Mel Yates; 114, 116–17 Paul Rivera; 118–119 Mel Yates; 120–21 Francis Amiand; 122 Mel Yates; 124–25 Paul Rivera; 126 Mel Yates; 127 CGI; 128 Mel Yates; 129 Paul Rivera; 130–31 Mel Yates; 132–33 CGI; 135, 136–37 Mel Yates; 138 Paul Rivera; 139 Claudia Uribe; 140 Courtesy of Kelly Hoppen Interiors; 142–43, 144–45, 146–47, 149 Mel Yates; 150–51 Francis Amiand; 152, 154 Mel Yates; 155 Paolo Feliciano for Century Properties Group Inc; 156–57 Mel Yates; 158 Francis Amiand; 159 Mel Yates; 160–61 Paolo Feliciano for Century Properties Group Inc; 162–63 Paul Rivera; 164–65, 167 Mel Yates; 168, 171, 172, 174–75, 177 Courtesy of Steve Leung; 178–79 Paolo Feliciano for Century Properties Group Inc; 180–81 CGI; 183 Gregor Titze; 184 Mel Yates; 185 Claudia Uribe; 186 Mel Yates; 187 Francis Amiand; 188–89, 190–91, 192–93 Mel Yates; 195 Francis Amiand; 196–97, 198–99 Mel Yates; 200 Claudia Uribe; 202–3 Mel Yates; 205 Francis Amiand; 206–7, 208 Mel Yates; 209 Francis Amiand; 210 Paolo Feliciano for Century Properties Group Inc; 211 Francis Amiand; 212–13 Mel Yates; 215, 216 Francis Amiand; 217 Paolo Feliciano for Century Properties Group Inc.